Cryptocurrency, DeFi and NFTs – 2 Books in 1

Discover the Trends that are Dominating this Market Cycle and Take Advantage of the Greatest Opportunity of the Century!

by Barry Johnson

The following Book is reproduced below with the goal of providing information that is as accurate and reliable as possible. Regardless, purchasing this Book can be seen as consent to the fact that both the publisher and the author of this book are in no way experts on the topics discussed within and that any recommendations or suggestions that are made herein are for entertainment purposes only. Professionals should be consulted as needed prior to undertaking any of the action endorsed herein. This declaration is deemed fair and valid by both the American Bar Association and the Committee of Publishers Association and is legally binding throughout the United States. Furthermore, the transmission, duplication, or reproduction of any of the following work including specific information will be considered an illegal act irrespective of if it is done electronically or in print. This extends to creating a secondary or tertiary copy of the work or a recorded copy and is only allowed with the express written consent from the Publisher. All additional rights reserved. The information in the following pages is broadly considered a truthful and accurate account of facts and as such, any inattention, use, or misuse of the information in question by

the reader will render any resulting actions solely under their purview. There are no scenarios in which the publisher or the original author of this work can be in any fashion deemed liable for any hardship or damages that may befall them after undertaking information described herein.

Additionally, the information in the following pages is intended only for informational purposes and should thus be thought of as universal. As befitting its nature, it is presented without assurance regarding its prolonged validity or interim quality. Trademarks that are mentioned are done without written consent and can in no way be considered an endorsement from the trademark holder.

Cryptocurrency Simply Explained!

The Only Investing Guide You Need to Master the World of Bitcoin and Blockchain – Discover the Secrets to Crypto Projects Like ADA, DOT, XRM, XRP and Flare!

by Barry Johnson

The following Book is reproduced below with the goal of providing information that is as accurate and reliable as possible. Regardless, purchasing this Book can be seen as consent to the fact that both the publisher and the author of this book are in no way experts on the topics discussed within and that any recommendations or suggestions that are made herein are for entertainment purposes only. Professionals should be consulted as needed prior to undertaking any of the action endorsed herein. This declaration is deemed fair and valid by both the American Bar Association and the Committee of Publishers Association and is legally binding throughout the United States. Furthermore, the transmission, duplication, or reproduction of any of the following work including specific information will be considered an illegal act irrespective of if it is done electronically or in print. This extends to creating a secondary or tertiary copy of the work or a recorded copy and is only allowed with the express written consent from the Publisher. All additional rights reserved. The information in the following pages is broadly considered a truthful and accurate account of facts and as such, any inattention, use, or misuse of the information in question by

the reader will render any resulting actions solely under their purview. There are no scenarios in which the publisher or the original author of this work can be in any fashion deemed liable for any hardship or damages that may befall them after undertaking information described herein.

Additionally, the information in the following pages is intended only for informational purposes and should thus be thought of as universal. As befitting its nature, it is presented without assurance regarding its prolonged validity or interim quality. Trademarks that are mentioned are done without written consent and can in no way be considered an endorsement from the trademark holder.

Table of Contents

Introduction

itcoin has taken the world by storm once again when it crossed \$20,000 per BTC in December of last year. After more than 2 years of bear market, the most famous cryptocurrency surpassed its previous all time high.

A lot of people are now trying to improvise themselves as professional investors and are losing a lot of money, only helping those who actually know what they are doing accumulate an incredible amount of wealth that will lead to generational fortunes.

To join the club of the few investors that actually make it, you need the right knowledge and the right mindset. Notice how we did not include a large initial capital. In fact, while having more money to invest means having more fire power, it is not necessary to have thousands of dollars to accumulate cryptocurrency and build wealth.

In fact, when we started investing in cryptocurrency we only had a few hundreds to put into the market, but that sum yielded us thousands and thousands of dollars over the span of a few years.

In this book you are going to discover everything there is to know about the fascinating world of cryptocurrency. From the operation of the Bitcoin blockchain to more advanced projects, like Uniswap and Compound.

If you diligently study the content of this book, we are sure you are going to see take your crypto knowledge to the next level. This also means you are going to see amazing results in a relative short period of time, since this bull run is offering an amazing number of opportunities.

To your success!

Barry Johnson

Chapter 1

Cardano (ADA)

Cardano and its related cryptocurrency ADA have attracted a lot of attention since its creation in 2015. The academic rigor applied to its development makes Cardano a rather unique project in the cryptocurrency industry.

The Cardano project is mainly developed by the technology company Input Output Hong Kong (IOHK), founded by Charles Hoskinson. Hoskinson also took part in the Ethereum development in its early days. But what is Cardano, and what are the features it plans to introduce in its long roadmap? Let's find out.

What is Cardano (ADA)?

Cardano is a multipurpose blockchain designed on the basis of academic research. Its development is entrusted to a multidisciplinary team of engineers, mathematicians, scientists and business experts.

The development of the platform is always achieved by applying a scientific approach. According to its creators, the fundamental design principles behind Cardano are security, scalability and interoperability. Ada, Cardano's native currency, is used to perform operations on the Cardano blockchain, in a relationship very similar to that between ether and Ethereum.

Cardano development is separated into multiple operating units. IOHK manages the development of the Cardano protocol, while the Cardano Foundation oversees the project and EMURGO is responsible for commercial development and adoption. IOHK also had to do with the development of Ethereum Classic (ETC).

The roadmap

Cardano's roadmap consists of five main stages: Byron, Shelley, Goguen, Basho and Voltaire. Byron, the first phase, saw the rollout of the network and core features, such as ADA relocations. The Shelley hard fork occurred in 2020 and offered further steps towards decentralization. Currently the nodes are operated by the Cardano community, with staking pools managed by ADA owners.

As of April 2021, the blockchain platform is still unable to accommodate functional smart contracts. According to the roadmap, this feature will be introduced with the Goguen update. Following Goguen, the Basho update will focus on optimizing scalability and interoperability, and the Voltaire update will introduce a treasury system to address the governance issue.

How Cardano works

Cardano is designed as a "third generation" blockchain, with the aim of solving the scalability problems of the first (e.g., Bitcoin) and second generation (e.g., Ethereum).

According to proponents of this classification, blockchains of previous generations suffer from bottlenecks that fundamentally limit the capacity they can handle. This makes them an inefficient choice for widespread use globally. We can observe the varying transaction times of BTC and ETH to confirm this problem.

In the documentation, Cardano indicates the computational power of VISA as a comparison: the network handles an average of 1,736 transactions per second (TPS) with the capacity to handle up to 24,000 TPS.

Cardano aims to improve capacity in several ways. One of the most significant pillars towards this goal is the Proof of Stake consensus mechanism called Ouroboros. Ouroboros reduces energy costs compared to Proof of Work and at the same time offers demonstrable safety guarantees.

Cardano's Layer 2 solution for further scalability, Hydra, is named after the mythological creature. The basic idea is that capacity increases with each new node added to the network.

The hard fork combiner is another key feature of Cardano, which allows you to hard fork without interruption or the need to restart the blockchain. The success of the Shelley update is proof of the effectiveness of this approach.

The key functions of Cardano

As we have mentioned, Cardano's strong points are its academic and scientific philosophy. The team developing Cardano has published more than 90 white papers for the underlying technology. The project has a well-defined roadmap, and the network aims to achieve high levels of security, scalability and interoperability.

Although not yet operational, the Cardano blockchain will introduce the functionality of scalable smart contracts in the future. Developed with VISA as a competitor and hardware limitations as a theoretical goal, Cardano could have all the elements needed to be used as a strong revolutionary fintech project.

As with Ethereum, the possibilities of Cardano's use cases are vast. The blockchain only aims to act as a foundation layer upon which to build applications.

Despite the great promises, Cardano has yet to meet expectations. That is something common to almost all projects in the crypto sector with the exception of Bitcoin. Even though Cardano is ambitious, its development is relatively slow.

The ADA Token

ADA is Cardano's token, named after 19th century mathematics Ada Lovelace. 57.6% of ADA's offering was distributed through an Initial Coin Offering (ICO), in which Cardano raised $62.2 million.
The token is both a digital currency and a way to transact on the Cardano network (similar to the role of ether to transact on Ethereum).

Additionally, ADA holders have a share of the Cardano network, which can be used in staking pools to generate rewards.

How to store ADA

Developed by IOHK, Daedalus is the open source desktop wallet software of choice for storing ADA. It is a full node wallet, so it is necessary to download the entire Cardano blockchain, and every transaction is verified for maximum user security.

Among the light wallets, which do not require you to download the entire blockchain, we find Yoroi Wallet and AdaLite. Additionally, it is possible to store ADA on hardware wallets such as Ledger and Trezor through Daedalus, Yoroi Wallet and AdaLite.

Will this third-generation blockchain project succeed in becoming the dominant smart contract platform, or will it arrive too late to the market? Are there 4th generation blockchains that offer better performance and functionality? These questions remain open as Cardano progresses on its roadmap.

What we know is that we have invested in ADA at 0.18$ and we have profit targets at $3 and $5.

Chapter 2

Polkadot (DOT)

Polkadot positions itself as the next generation blockchain protocol, capable of linking multiple specialized blockchains into a universal network. With a strong focus on developing the Web 3.0 infrastructure Polkadot aims to destroy internet monopolies and distribute power into the hands of individual users.

While the blockchain has been called a revolutionary technology, there are undoubtedly disadvantages to be taken into consideration. Individual blockchains are unable to communicate with each other. Introducing interoperability between different chains could lead to data exchange and potentially more powerful applications and services.

In the past, developers have tried to "link" different blockchains. This process allows chain A to work with chain B and vice versa. However, connecting many blockchains at the same time remains an unsolved problem. The Polkadot team, and by extension the Web3 Foundation, are convinced that an elegant solution can be created in the coming years.

What is Polkadot?

Described as an open source protocol built for everyone, Polkadot claims to be the next step in the evolution of blockchain technology. It is a concept originally envisioned by Dr. Gavin Wood, the co-founder of Ethereum. The team wants to focus on security, scalability and innovation. To do this, the necessary infrastructure must be created not only to support new ideas and concepts, but to ensure adequate interoperability as well.

An individual blockchain in the Polkadot ecosystem is called a parachain, while the main blockchain is called the Relay Chain. The idea is that the parachains and the Relay Chain can easily exchange information at any time. You can think of parachains as similar to individual shards in the planned implementation of ETH 2.0.

Any developer, company or individual can launch their own custom parachain through Substrate, a framework for creating cryptocurrencies and decentralized systems. Once the custom blockchain is connected to the Polkadot network, it becomes interoperable with all other parachains on the network.

Building cross-chain applications, products and services should become an easier process with this design. So far, cross-blockchain transfers of data or assets have not been possible on a large scale.

The protection and validation of data across these different parachains is done through network validators, and a small group of these validators can protect multiple parachains. Furthermore, these validators ensure that transactions can be spread across various parachains to improve scalability.

The advantages of Polkadot

There are several reasons for developers to explore the Polkadot ecosystem. Due to the limited nature of current blockchains, it is clear that there are fundamental problems to be addressed: scalability, customization, interoperability, governance and upgradeability.

On the scalability front, Polkadot offers several features. It acts as a multichain network, allowing users to process transfers in parallel across several individual chains. This removes one of the major hurdles associated with blockchain technology today. Parallel processing is a significant improvement and can pave the way for wider global blockchain adoption.

Those looking for customization can take advantage of other features provided by Polkadot. At present, there is no "one blockchain infrastructure to tame them all". Each project has individual needs and requirements, and Polkadot allows each individual chain to optimize its design for this specific functionality. With the help of Substrate, developers can efficiently tailor their individual blockchains to meet the needs of the project.

When it comes to interoperability, the smooth sharing of data between projects and applications is an important factor. While it remains to be seen what kind of products and services this system will create, there are plenty of possible use cases. It can create a whole new financial ecosystem, with each individual parachain dealing with a particular aspect of the system.

Any community associated with a specific parachain will be able to manage their network as they see fit. Furthermore, all communities are crucial for the future governance of Polkadot as a whole. Collecting feedback from the community can provide valuable information to evolve projects over time.

Plus, Polkadot makes upgrading individual parachains really easy. There is no need for hard forks, as these events can divide communities. Instead, the native chain can be upgraded without friction.

The DOT token

Similar to most other blockchain infrastructure projects, Polkadot has its own native token. Known as DOT, it acts as a network token, just like ETH is the token of Ethereum and BTC is the token of Bitcoin.

This token carries out several use cases. First of all, it grants owners governance rights over the entire Polkadot platform. This includes setting commissions, votes on general network updates, and the launch or removal of parachain.

DOT is also designed to facilitate network consensus through staking. Similar to other networks that take advantage of the staking mechanism, all DOT holders are incentivized to follow the rules at any time. If they don't, they could lose their stake.

The third function of the token is bonding. This process is necessary when new parachains are added to the Polkadot ecosystem. During the bonding period, the involved DOTs are locked, and released at the end of the bond duration when the parachain is removed from the ecosystem.

Staking and bonding on Polkadot

Polkadot's approach to interoperability goes far beyond the simple exchange of data and assets. It is also a way to introduce new concepts, such as incentivizing honest token staking and bonding.

Staking of tokens on a blockchain network is not a new concept. Known as Proof of Stake, this consensus model works by rewarding users for staking coins on the network. With Polkadot, honest stakers are rewarded, while bad operators can lose the entire stake.

As we mentioned before, each new parachain is added through DOT token bonding. Bonding refers to blocking tokens on the network for a specific period of time. Unnecessary chains or abandoned projects will be removed, and locked tokens will be returned.

On paper, there are many things that make Polkadot attractive in the eyes of developers. It is an ecosystem dedicated to individual programmers, small businesses and large corporations. Having the ability to implement custom blockchains to meet specific needs, and update them seamlessly, is a new concept that could be invaluable to the entire crypto industry.

That said, Polkadot remains a very young ecosystem. Even though several projects are already under development, it will take some time before the first major blockchains are launched. According to PolkaProject, there are hundreds of projects under development, from wallets to infrastructure projects, tools, dApps and more.

As for DOT, the creators of Polkadot have stated that it is not a token intended for speculation. While it has monetary value on exchanges, it is primarily designed for the purposes we just described.

We have purchased DOT at $6 and it represents around 10% of our portfolio.

Chapter 3

Ripple (XRP)

Previously known as OpenCoin, Ripple is a private company that is creating a payment and exchange network (RippleNet) on a distributed database ledger (XRP Ledger). Ripple's core purpose is to connect banks, payment service providers and digital asset exchanges, making global payments faster and more cost-effective.

The history of Ripple

Ripple was created in 2004 by Ryan Fugger, who developed the first prototype of Ripple as a decentralized digital money system (RipplePay). The system was inaugurated in 2005 and aimed to provide secure payment solutions within a global network.

In 2012, Fugger sold the project to Jed McCaleb and Chris Larsen, who founded the American technology company OpenCoin. Since then, Ripple has started to be developed as a protocol focused on payment solutions for banks and other financial institutions. In 2013, OpenCoin was renamed with the Ripple Labs brand, turning into Ripple in 2015.

The XRP Ledger

Building on Fugger's work and inspired by the creation of Bitcoin, in 2012 Ripple introduced the Ripple Consensus Ledger (RCL), along with its native cryptocurrency XRP. The RCL was later renamed XRP Ledger (XRPL).

XRPL acts as a distributed economic system that not only keeps all the accounting information of the network participants but also offers exchange services between different currency pairs. Ripple presents XRPL as an open source distributed ledger that allows for real-time financial transactions. These transactions are protected and verified by the network participants through a consensus mechanism.

However, unlike Bitcoin, XRP Ledger does not rely on a Proof of Work consensus algorithm and, as a result, does not use a mining process to verify transactions. The network achieves consensus through the use of a custom consensus algorithm. This algorithm is formerly known as the Ripple Protocol Consensus Algorithm (RPCA).

XRPL is managed by a network of independent validation nodes that constantly compare their operation logs. Anyone can start and manage a Ripple validation node and choose which nodes to trust as validators. However, Ripple recommends its customers to use a list of identified and trusted participants to validate their transactions. This list is known as the Unique Node List (UNL).

The nodes of the UNL transfer transaction data between them until everyone agrees on the current state of the register. In other words, transactions that are accepted by a large majority of UNL nodes are considered valid and consensus is reached when all of these nodes add the same set of transactions to the ledger.

According to the official website, Ripple is a private company that funded the development of XRPL as an open source distributed ledger. This means that anyone can contribute to the code and that XRPL would be able to continue even if the company ceases to exist.

RippleNet

Unlike XRPL, RippleNet is exclusive to the Ripple company and was developed on top of XRPL as a payment and exchange network.

RippleNet currently offers a 3-product suite designed as a payment system for banks and other financial institutions. These products are xRapid, xCurrent, and xVia.

xRapid

In short, xRapid is an on-demand liquidity solution that uses XRP as an intermediate currency between different fiat currencies. Both XRP and xRapid are based on the XRP Ledger, which offers faster confirmation times and much lower rates than conventional methods.

Let's make a simple example. Bob is in Australia and wants to send $100 to Alice in India. Bob transfers the money through a financial institution called FIN. To carry out the transaction, FIN uses the xRapid solution to create a connection with exchanges in the countries of origin and destination. By doing so, the company is able to convert Bob's $100 into XRP, providing the necessary liquidity for the final payment. Within seconds, XRPs are converted to Indian Rupees and Alice can withdraw the money from an exchange in India. As you can imagine, if Bob and Alice followed the standard path of wire transfers, the transaction would have been much slower and more expensive.

xCurrent

xCurrent is a solution developed to provide instant transaction settlement and international payment tracking between RippleNet members. Unlike xRapid, the xCurrent solution is not based on the XRP Ledger and does not use the XRP cryptocurrency by default.

xCurrent is built on the Interledger Protocol (ILP), designed by Ripple to connect different registers or payment networks.

The four basic components of xCurrent are the following.

- **Messenger**. xCurrent messenger provides peer-to-peer communication between financial institutions connected through RippleNet. It is used to exchange information relating to risk and compliance, rates, exchange rates, payment details and expected times for the disbursement of funds.

- **Validator**. Validator is used to cryptographically confirm the success or failure of a transaction, as well as to coordinate the movement of funds in the Interledger. Financial institutions can run their own validator or rely on a third party.

- **ILP Ledger**. The Interledger Protocol is implemented within existing bank registers, creating the ILP Ledger. The ILP Ledger acts as a sub-ledger and is used to track credits, debts and liquidity through the parties carrying out transactions. Funds are settled automatically.

- **FX Ticker**. The FX ticker is used to define the exchange rates between the parties to the transactions. It monitors the current status of each configured Ledger ILP.

Even though xCurrent was designed primarily for fiat currencies, it also supports cryptocurrency transactions.

xVia

xVia is a standardized API-based interface that allows banks and other financial service providers to interact within a single facility, without having to rely on various payment network integrations. xVia allows banks to create payments through other credit partners connected to RippleNet, and also allows them to attach invoices or other information to transactions.

While Bitcoin is known as the open cryptocurrency and Ethereum is famous for creating a global smart contract platform, we can consider the Ripple network as a monetary exchange system that focuses on global payment solutions for banks and other financial institutions.

RippleNet can be implemented on top of the existing banking infrastructure as a means to complement and improve the traditional payment system. xCurrent allows for cost-effective and real-time payments through financial institutions, xRapid uses XRP as an intermediate currency to provide on-demand liquidity funds, and xVia facilitates the integration and communication of all RippleNet participants.

Chapter 4

Flare and Spark (FLR)

Flare is a distributed network with some unique properties. It can be used to build two-way bridges between networks, such as Ethereum and XRP Ledger. This means that it allows you to use the XRP token within smart contracts.

Spark Token is Flare's native token. A portion of the offering will be distributed to XRP holders through an airdrop.

As you should know by now, Ripple's XRP Ledger (XRPL) is a global payment and exchange network. Being optimized for this use case, it offers limited utility with regards to other kinds of functionality.

This is what the Flare Network aims to solve by introducing smart contract support for the XRP token.

Spark is the native token of this network, and a portion of its offering will be distributed to eligible XRP holders. Let's find out how it works.

What Flare Network is

The Flare Network is a distributed network that integrates the Ethereum Virtual Machine (EVM). Essentially, the EVM converts smart contracts into instructions that computers can read. This allows the network to execute complete Turing smart contracts. This attribute means that it can perform virtually any computational task, as long as there is enough memory to do so.

As a result, it can combine important properties to create an ecosystem of decentralized applications. In short, Flare aims to offer scalability for smart contract networks.

Flare uses a consensus protocol called Avalanche, which has been adapted to work with the Federated Byzantine Agreement (FBA). FBA is a consensus mechanism used by networks like XRPL and Stellar.

We won't go into detail in this chapter, the point is that Flare's consensus algorithm doesn't rely on economic mechanisms like Proof of Stake to maintain network security.

You may be wondering, what are these economic mechanisms? Let's take for example a token like ether (ETH) for the Ethereum network. When Ethereum completes its Proof of Stake (PoS) transition with Ethereum 2.0, network security will completely depend on validators staking their tokens. This means that, by extension, security will depend on the token. The consensus protocol implemented by Flare does not provide for this measure.

Why should this be emphasized? Because it allows the network token to be used for other kinds of applications. Even some that would be dangerous for networks that rely on the token for security. In practice, according to the creators of Flare, this design choice adds greater versatility to the token without compromising its security.

What is FLR?

Spark is the native token of the Flare Network. Its basic use case is similar to that of other native tokens, preventing spam attacks. If the transactions were free, even spamming and congesting the network with useless transactions would cost nothing.

Additionally, Spark Token can be used for the following features:

- As a collateral in decentralized applications (dApps)
- To provide data to an on-chain oracle
- To participate in the governance of the protocol

These three components aim to enable an ecosystem of Spark-based applications called Spark Dependent Application (SDA). Additionally, SDAs allow trustless representations of tokens on other networks, even those that do not natively support smart contracts. Are you starting to guess where we are getting? Yes, this is where XRP comes in.

What is the FXRP token?

FXRP is a trustless representation of the XRP token on the Flare Network. It can be created and redeemed by XRP owners through smart contracts.

The system relies on participants pledging Spark Token as collateral and earning commissions for creating and redeeming FXRP. This, combined with potential arbitrage opportunities, should ensure that the 1: 1 ratio between XRP and FXRP is maintained.
We mentioned that Flare allows you to use smart contracts on networks that don't support them. This is exactly the goal of FXRP. It allows XRP to be used in smart contracts without the need for a central authority to issue wrapped tokens. In other words, in a trustless way.

The Flare Network is a new scaling solution for networks that don't support smart contracts. Flare allows you to use XRP in smart contracts in a trustless way.

Chapter 5

Monero (XMR)

Public blockchains are inherently transparent. For blockchains to work in a decentralized environment, each participant must be able to independently verify all of their transactions. A quick glance at Bitcoin or Ethereum is enough to see how public their databases are.

Such an infrastructure offers several benefits, but it often does so at the expense of privacy and anonymity. Observers can link transactions and addresses in the blockchain to potentially deanonymize address owners.

These so-called pseudonymous cryptocurrencies are useful for a myriad of applications. However, privacy coins may be more desirable for those seeking true financial privacy. And when it comes to private cryptocurrencies, few have the same reputation as Monero.

What is Monero?

Monero is a cryptocurrency created according to the principles of non-associability and non-traceability. In simpler terms, this means that it shouldn't be possible to link two Monero transactions, nor to determine the source or destination of the funds.

This is what sets Monero apart from the rest of cryptocurrencies. It always uses a blockchain to track the movements of funds, but applies an interesting cryptographic scheme to obscure the sources, amounts and destinations of transactions.

A brief history of Monero

Monero is a fork of Bytecoin, a privacy-oriented cryptocurrency released in 2012. Bytecoin was the first protocol based on CryptoNote, an open source technology with the aim of solving some of the flaws of

Bitcoin. We are referring to ASIC mining and the lack of privacy in transactions. CryptoNote now forms the basis of many cryptocurrencies that want to value confidentiality.

In 2014, developers dissatisfied with Bytecoin's initial distribution forked the coin into a new project known as Bitmonero. Later, the name was changed in Monero.

How does Monero work?

While researching Monero, it is easy to come across the terms "ring signature" and "stealth addresses". These are two of the main innovations behind the anonymity of Monero's transactions. In this chapter, we will provide an overview of both concepts.

Ring signatures and confidential transactions

A ring signature is a type of digital signature created by someone in a specified group. With the signature and public keys of the group members available, anyone can verify that one of the participants provided the signature. However, it is not possible to understand which of these provided it.

In 2001, the "How to Leak a Secret" document illustrated this concept using the example of a government cabinet. Suppose a member of this cabinet - Bob - has incriminating evidence on the Prime Minister. Bob wants to prove to a reporter that he really is a cabinet member, but he wants to remain anonymous.

Bob would not be able to do this with a normal digital signature. Comparing it to his public key, anyone could confidently claim that only Bob's private key could have produced the signature. He could suffer serious consequences for spying on the Prime Minister's activities. However, by using the keys of the other cabinet members in a ring signature scheme, it will not be possible to determine which of them sent the message. However, it will be possible to say with certainty that the information comes from a cabinet member, thus proving its authenticity.

This technique is used every time you create a transaction, giving you anonymity. During the construction of the transaction, your Monero wallet takes other users' keys from the blockchain to form a ring. These keys actually act as diversions. To an observer, it will appear that anyone in the ring may have signed your transaction. Consequently, a stranger will never be able to determine whether an output has been spent or not. At best, they may know that one of the eight outputs shown in the image below may have been spent. We call the number of diversion outputs mixin.

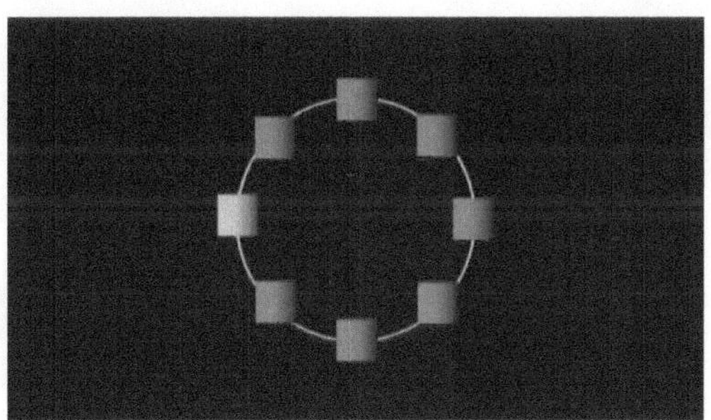

In the image above, the green output is what you are really spending, and the red ones are the diversions you have collected from the blockchain.

In the past, the outputs included in the ring had to be the same size. Otherwise, it would have been easy to understand what was going on, as the transaction amounts were visible. For example, you might have seen a ring that included only 2 XMR outputs or one where only 0.5 XMR outputs were included.

The update to RingCT (Ring Confidential Transactions) changed that. It has integrated confidential transactions, a technique in which transaction amounts are not visible. This integration into the Monero protocol has been a big boost in terms of privacy. You can now build a ring with outputs of various sizes without revealing information that could be used to de-anonymize you.

Stealth addresses

Ring signatures hide where the funds are coming from, but with regular public addresses you would still be able to see where they are going. This could be problematic if your identity is linked to one of your blockchain addresses.

Let's say we use the same address in our e-commerce store for every order. Anyone who buys on our site can see the balance we have and tell others that this is our business address. This could make us a target.

Stealth addresses hide the destination of funds. Essentially, the sender generates a one-time address based on a public address used only for that transaction. The public address might look like this:

41mT1gUnYHK6mDAxVsKeB7SP9hVesbESbWcupd7 mMYC73GL4nSgsEwTGKHGT7GKoSEdMKvs8Fdu1uf PJbo5BV4d1PfYiEew

If you search for the address in a Monero block explorer, you will see that you cannot link any transactions to it. When a sender wants to send you funds, they create a stealth address by passing the above address through some math function. When they send XMR, they send it to a new address on the blockchain. Each address created will be different from the previous one, and cannot be connected to it.

However, there are two pieces of information you can use: the "view private key" and the spend private key. As the name indicates, the "view key" allows you to see all transactions associated with your address. You can give it to others to check the funds you have received. The spend key is what we usually think of as our private key. You use it to spend your coins.

Monero has a default privacy policy, meaning you can't decide not to use a stealth address. Therefore, while the public ledger is automatically blacked out, you can still make your transactions transparent to participants of your choice.

Monero vs. Bitcoin

Monero and Bitcoin have some similarities, but in reality they both have many unique aspects. Let's take a look at them.

Fungibility

Fungibility is a source of controversial discussions in the field of Bitcoin. It refers to the interchangeability of an asset with another asset of a similar type. Gold, for example, is considered fungible because you can trade one ounce of your own for someone else's, and this will be functionally identical. The same goes for coins and banknotes. You can exchange one ten-dollar bill for another. On the contrary, a unique masterpiece like the Mona Lisa is not fungible as there is no other similar unit.

In many digital currencies, determining fungibility appears to be more complicated. Bitcoin units are fungible at the protocol level, as the software makes no distinction between units of BTC. The situation becomes more ambiguous on a social and political level. Some argue that Bitcoin is not fungible because each output is unique, while others argue that this doesn't matter.

Since the Bitcoin blockchain is transparent, transaction details, such as amounts and recipients, can be tracked. Suppose you receive a five-dollar bill as change in a grocery store. Ten transactions prior to this, the note may have been used in a criminal transaction, which would have no effect on its current usability. With Bitcoin, we have seen occasions where some coins have been rejected or confiscated based on their "dirty" history. Even if users are unaware of previous transactions, surveillance services that analyze the blockchain can blacklist certain coins and affect their usability as a currency. And this is why some consider Bitcoin a non-fungible asset.

The "clean" coins, i.e. those that have just been mined, could be seen as more valuable than the old and "dirtier" ones.

Opponents of coin profiling believe that this practice uses unreliable and subjective techniques for analysis. In fact, several tools for mixing and CoinJoining are increasingly accessible to average users, and allow you to obfuscate the source of your funds.

Monero eliminates these problems right from the start. Since observers cannot know where the funds are coming from or where they are going, it is perhaps more like cash than non-privacy coins can be. Even in businesses with strict analytics policies, XMRs from suspicious transactions can be traded without any problems.

Monero's added privacy comes at a price though. Transactions are much larger. Therefore, there are major hurdles to overcome before the system can expand and scale to accommodate the masses.
Curiously, its strong fungibility has given the cryptocurrency a certain degree of notoriety, surpassing Bitcoin as the currency of choice for cybercriminals involved in cryptojacking, ransomware and dark web transactions.

Blocks and mining

Like Bitcoin, Monero uses Proof-of-Work to add transaction blocks to the blockchain. However, like all CryptoNote-based protocols, it is designed to be ASIC-resistant. The goal of this property is to prevent domain mining pools that use specialized high-performance hardware mining.

Monero's Proof-of-Work algorithm aims to make the system fairer by favoring CPU mining and weakening the effectiveness of GPUs. The rationale behind this measure is that mining will be better distributed as common PCs continue to be competitive. Despite this, hashing power remains relatively concentrated in a handful of mining pools.

As for the block size, Monero does not have a fixed limit, unlike the 4 million units by weight of the Bitcoin block. Instead, it has a dynamic block size. This means blocks can expand to accommodate greater demand. Likewise, if demand falls, the permitted size will decrease. The dimensions are calculated considering the average size of the previous hundred blocks. Miners can produce blocks that exceed the limit, but will be penalized with a reduced reward.

Importantly, the supply is not limited, as is the case with Bitcoin. Monero also has a decreasing block reward program, but it doesn't tend towards zero. Instead, the subsidy will remain indefinitely at a fixed amount to incentivize participants in block mining.

Hard fork

We find another interesting difference between Bitcoin and Monero at the governance level. Bitcoin is quite averse to forks, to the point that even simple updates remain under discussion for a long time before being implemented. But there is a reason for this. In fact, Bitcoin developers have to be cautious to ensure the system remains stable, secure, and decentralized.

Of course, forks are just protocol update mechanisms. They are often needed to fix critical bugs or to add new features. However, in Bitcoin users prefer to avoid them as they can cause divisions, and could pose a threat to decentralization. Typically, Bitcoin hard forks emerge when a group wants to create a new cryptocurrency from the existing network. Outside of this, they are usually reserved for emergency cases where urgent vulnerabilities need to be addressed.

In the case of Monero the roadmap has frequent hard forks. This ensures that the software can quickly adapt to changes and integrate security updates. Some see "mandatory" protocol updates as a weakness, even though Monero's hard forks don't carry negative connotations like other cryptocurrencies. This does not mean that they are foolproof. In fact, frequent hard forks increase the risk of undetected vulnerabilities, and can push out-of-date users off the network.

Monero development

Monero development is open to everyone. Anyone can contribute to the source code and documentation. The community decides which features to add, remove or modify. At the time of writing, the project has more than 500 collaborators. The Core development team is made up of developers such as Riccardo Spagni (aka FluffyPony), Francisco Cabañas (ArticMine) and the pseudonymous devs NoodleDoodle, Othe and binaryFate.

In addition to sponsorships, the development is funded by the Community Crowdfunding System. Users can propose ideas which, if selected by the community, follow a crowdfunding period. When certain milestones are reached the funds are distributed to the managers.

For years, Monero has been the go-to cryptocurrency for those looking for strong privacy guarantees. It has a dedicated community of developers who work to increase the confidentiality of user transactions. The new updates aim to further the mission of providing non-associable and non-traceability in cryptocurrencies.

We have invested in XRM in 2017 and we are holding it for the long term. We encourage you to look into it, as it is a pretty interesting project.

Chapter 6

Binance Smart Chain (BSC)

Binance Chain was launched by Binance in April 2019. Its primary goal is to facilitate fast and decentralized trading. Perhaps unsurprisingly, the largest decentralized application built on top of it is Binance DEX, one of the most accessible decentralized exchanges on the market. You can use it through a web interface at binance.org or through its native integration with Trust Wallet.

However, due to the inherent limitations of blockchain-based systems, Binance Chain does not have much flexibility to introduce smart contracts into a system optimized for real-time trading that could significantly congest the network. Have you heard of CryptoKitties? At the peak of its popularity, it brought the Ethereum blockchain to complete paralysis.

Scalability remains one of the most important challenges for blockchain development. And this is where Binance Smart Chain comes into play.

What is Binance Smart Chain?

Binance Smart Chain (BSC) can be described as a blockchain operating in parallel with Binance Chain. Unlike the latter, BSC offers smart contract functionality and compatibility with the Ethereum Virtual Machine. The design goal was to leave Binance Chain's high capabilities intact while introducing smart contracts into its ecosystem.

In essence, both blockchains operate side by side. BSC is not a layer two or off-chain scaling solution, but an independent blockchain that can work even if the Binance Chain goes offline. That said, both systems bear a strong design similarity.

Since BSC is compatible with EVM, it was launched with support from the rich universe of Ethereum tools and dApps. In theory, this makes it easier for developers to transfer their projects from Ethereum. For users, it means that applications like MetaMask can be easily configured to work with BSC. Seriously, it's just a matter of changing a couple of settings.

How Binance Smart Chain works

Binance Smart Chain achieves 3 second block times with a Proof-of-Stake consensus algorithm. Specifically, it uses a model called Proof of Staked Authority (or PoSA), where participants staking BNB to become validators. If they propose a valid block, they receive the transaction fees included in it.

Unlike many protocols, rewards are not distributed in newly issued BNB, as BNB is not inflationary. Conversely, the supply of BNB decreases over time as the Binance team carries out coin burns periodically.

Cross-chain compatibility

Binance Smart Chain was conceived as an independent system but complementary to the existing Binance Chain. Dual-chain architecture is used, to allow users to easily transfer assets from one blockchain to another. In this way, Binance Chain can offer fast trading, while powerful decentralized apps can be built on BSC. With this interoperability, users have a vast ecosystem at their disposal that can accommodate a number of use cases.

Binance Chain's BEP-2 and BEP-8 tokens can be exchanged for BEP-20 tokens, the new standard introduced for Binance Smart Chain.

To move tokens from one chain to another (from BEP-2 to BEP-20 or vice versa), the easiest method is to use the Binance Chain Wallet, available on Chrome and Firefox.

Decentralized Finance on Binance Smart Chain

You may already know that several digital assets - such as BTC, LTC, ETH, EOS and XRP - already exist on Binance Chain as "Peggy coins." These are tokens anchored to assets on their respective native chains. For example, you might decide to block 10 BTC in order to receive 10 BTCB on the Binance Chain. At any time, you can trade your 10 BTCB for 10 BTC, so the BTCB price should closely follow that of the native BTC.

By doing so, you are effectively transferring these assets to the Binance Chain. This is a type of tokenization and you should be familiar with this concept if you have read the dedicated chapter.

Thanks to the flexibility offered by the Binance Smart Chain, assets from a number of different chains can be used in the emerging DeFi industry. For example, applications like PancakeSwap allow users to trade assets trustlessly, participate in yield farming, and vote on proposals. Similar projects include BurgerSwap and BakerySwap.

Binance Smart Chain vastly expands the functionality of the original Binance Chain and joins a number of cutting-edge protocols designed to bridge the gap between different blockchains. While still in its early stages, the platform is an ideal engine for developers who want to build useful decentralized applications.

Chapter 7

Staking BNB on the Binance Smart Chain

Binance Smart Chain allows you to use the unlimited DeFi infrastructure at low cost. It is managed by a set of 21 community validator nodes that process transactions, provide processing power and hardware, ensuring network security. In return, they receive rewards from BNB's transaction fees and staking.

The purpose of the validators is to make BSC a bigger and more accessible ecosystem.

Validators

Binance Smart Chain uses a consensus model called Proof of Staked Authority (PoSA). It is a hybrid between the Proof of Authority (PoA) and the Delegated Proof of Stake (DPoS). This consensus model supports faster block times, lower fees, and ultimately requires only 21 validators to run.

Validators take turns producing the new blocks, feeding the BSC network through transaction processing and signing the blocks. In exchange for their service, they earn a reward in BNB tokens. In the meantime, they need daily re-election in order to continue being part of the set of validators; this is based on the amount of BNB they hold in stake.

What are the requirements to become a validator? A validator must maintain a node with the required specifications, manage a full BSC node and stake at least 10,000 BNBs. But that is not all. These requirements are only sufficient to become an elected candidate.

To actually start producing new blocks, a validator candidate must become a selected validator. The selected validators are the first 21 candidate validators with the most voting power. They change every 24 hours through a continuous election process and you can check them on the list of top validators on Binance.org.

What is a delegate on Binance Smart Chain (BSC)?

Becoming a validator isn't for everyone, so how can you participate as an ordinary user? Well, you can become a delegate and stake your BNBs to candidate validators using one of the supported wallets. Through staking, you can choose your favorite validators and help them achieve the minimum stake requirements required by the protocol.

In short, you are pooling your BNBs with your favorite validator. As we know, validators receive a reward in BNB. In exchange for the staking vote, the validator shares a portion of their earnings with their delegates. Therefore, we have a win-win situation for both parts.

Furthermore, delegates can transfer part of their staked BNB to another validator. This process is called redelegation. Redelegation is a great way to support multiple validators at the same time.

Delegates can also de-stake their BNBs. This function is called undelegate. As you guessed, this eliminates the delegation towards the selected validators. Note that the un-delegation requires an unbonding period of 7 days, at the end of which the delegate receives the BNBs that they had staked. During this phase the delegate does not receive any reward in BNB.

Should you become a delegate on Binance Smart Chain (BSC)?

The choice is yours. By becoming a delegate, you are delegating your staked BNBs to your favorite validator. Additionally, you are entrusting them with your voting power to approve or disapprove governance decisions. Furthermore, validators can control certain functionalities on BSC, such as adjusting gas prices, changing system parameters or even updating the blockchain.

By delegating your BNB to a validator, you will also increase its stake in relation to the total reward pool. Both of you, by joining forces, earn advantages and a reward. As of February 2021, the average daily reward for a validator on BSC was 134 BNB. Meanwhile, the average APR for delegates on BSC was 60%.

While the economic incentives are great and make everything work smoothly, being a delegate isn't all about returns. By becoming a delegate, you are directly supporting BSC's operations and security.

How to become a validator on Binance Smart Chain (BSC)

To become a BSC validator, you must meet these requirements:

- have powerful hardware;
- run a full node BSC;
- stake at least 10,000 BNB.

This will allow you to enter the list of candidate validators and potentially attract more delegates to stake their BNBs to your validator node.

As of April 2021, the top 21 elected validators all have more than 150,000 BNB staked. Therefore, there will be a lot of competition in the coming months, as the price of the BNB token increases.

How to become a delegate on Binance Smart Chain (BSC)

Becoming a delegate is probably the best choice if you want to avoid all the technical aspects of the validator. If you are a BNB owner, delegating your stake can be a simple solution to supporting BSC and earning a profit.

You can check out these guides on how to stake your BNBs using the most popular wallets:

- Binance Chain Wallet
- Trust Wallet
- MathWallet

Stake interest is distributed to the delegate every day after 00:00 UTC. When you delegate your stake to a validator, you will start receiving rewards the second day after delegating.

As of April 2021 the best validator has an APR of 27%. Not bad, but remember that rewards can fluctuate over time.

Whether you are a developer, a user or just a DeFi enthusiast, there are many ways to participate in the development of the BSC ecosystem. BNB staking is a great way to participate in BSC as a direct advocate of network health and safety.

We stake our BNB tokens with different validators and they have proved to be a nice source of income. We definitely recommend this practice.

Chapter 8

BakerySwap

BakerySwap is a DeFi protocol developed on Binance Smart Chain that offers interesting rewards. It works as a decentralized exchange by adopting the automated market maker model.

You've probably seen a ton of food-themed projects in the DeFi industry before. All of these protocols share one feature: users provide liquidity and earn tokens as a reward.

While many may associate DeFi with the Ethereum blockchain, more and more projects are being launched on Binance Smart Chain due to its minimal fees and faster confirmation times.

In this chapter, we will take a look at BakerySwap. It is a decentralized exchange built on the Binance Smart Chain.

What BakerySwap is

BakerySwap is a decentralized exchange that adopts the automated market maker model popularized by Uniswap.

BakerySwap is one of the first projects to leverage BSC to develop a DEX AMM. Furthermore, it is one of the few DeFi projects on Binance Smart Chain to offer liquidity pools for altcoins.

As with other platforms that use the AMM model, there is no order book to match buyers and sellers. Instead, users trade against a liquidity pool. The assets in each pool are provided by BakerySwap supporters and users.

Users who add liquidity to these pools receive liquidity provider tokens in exchange, based on their share of the pool. Later, they can convert these LP tokens to the original tokens they provided. The amount received also depends on the respective share of the pool. As a reward for the liquidity provided, they earn trading fees.

The BAKE farming process

As you'd expect from a platform called BakerySwap, the native token is called BAKE. You can earn it by staking BAKE, or by providing liquidity to one of the pools and staking your liquidity pool tokens.

For example, if you provide liquidity to the DOT-BNB pool, you will receive DOT-BNB BLP tokens. After that, you can stake these BLP tokens to receive BAKE. If you want to simply buy BAKE on the market instead of farming it, you can do it as well. Let's take a deeper look at the platform.

BakerySwap's liquidity pools

On BakerySwap, BAKE token stakers can explore pastry-themed menus. If you select Bread, you can stake BAKE to earn more BAKE. Alternatively, you can stake matching BLP tokens in pools, such as Donuts, Waffles, Rolls, Croissants, and so on. Remember that the potential ROI is different for each option.

As of April 2021, supported BEP-20 liquidity pools are the following.

- Bread: Staking by BAKE to earn BAKE
- Donut: Staking of BAKE-BNB BLP to earn BAKE
- Waffle: Staking by BAKE-BUSD BLP to earn BAKE
- Rolls: BUSD-BNB BLP staking to earn BAKE
- Croissant: Staking of BAKE-DOT BLP to earn BAKE
- Milk: USDT-BUSD BLP staking to earn BAKE
- Toast: Staking ETH-BNB BLP to earn BAKE
- Cake: Staking BTC-BNB BLP to earn BAKE

How to use BakerySwap

When you visit the BakerySwap website, you need to connect an eligible wallet to unlock all features. We recommend using MetaMask. MetaMask is an Ethereum wallet, but it can support Binance Smart Chain and its dApps with ease.

Once everything is set up, you can unlock the wallet to reveal additional information on the website.

Adding liquidity

The process of adding liquidity to BakerySwap is not very different from that of Uniswap or similar platforms. First of all you need to add liquidity to the DEX and provide both tokens to participate in that specific liquidity pool. Once liquidity is provided, you can start farming with BAKE.

To add liquidity, click on Exchange in the top menu and select the Pool tab. Then, click the "Add Liquidity" button.

Now, select the token pair you want to provide liquidity to. For example, you can select BNB and BAKE, so you will receive BAKE-BNB BLP tokens in return.

Once you have received your BLP tokens, you should navigate to "Earning" and select the option that corresponds to your BLP tokens. In this example, you will select Donut.

At this point, you should enter the amount of tokens you want to stake and confirm the transaction. Once completed, you can leave the page. You can come back at any time to see how many BAKEs you have earned. Received BAKEs are automatically collected when you withdraw the BLP token. Also, you can manually collect them by clicking on the Harvest button.

Other functions

We talked about the basic functionality offered by BakerySwap. But it doesn't stop there. There are other unique features to try.

One of these is the NFT marketplace, which allows you to buy non-fungible tokens.

Another unique feature is the BakerySwap Launchpad. It is a place where you can access newly launched projects on BSC. However, unlike Binance Launchpad, these are not "normal" tokens, they are NFTs.

The first Initial Dex Offering (IDO) was Battle Pets, a blockchain-based fighting game where players can breed, trade, and compete with NFT animals on the Binance Smart Chain.

The BakerySwap NFT Combo pool

In addition to this, BakerySwap allows you to create special menus called NFT Combo. These tools require you to lock BAKE and involve a bit of randomness. The more BAKE you block, the higher the class of NFT Combo you can create. These combos give you more and more Staking Power to earn more BAKE by farming your BLP tokens.

You can break them down at any time and take back 90% of the blocked BAKEs to create them. However, at the time of writing, all NFT Combo have been sold.

There are four classes of NFT Combo, and each requires a different amount of BAKE.

- Basic: 10,000–20,000 BAKE
- Regular: 20,000–50,000 BAKE
- Luxury: 50,000–100,000 BAKE
- Supreme: Over 100,000 BAKE

Remember, the Staking Power you receive for each combo is unique. It is based on the amount of BAKE you have blocked and a random multiplier. Therefore, the more BAKE you block, the higher your Staking Power potential will be.

Is BakerySwap Safe?

So far, there have been no reported problems with BakerySwap. An audit of the BakerySwap smart contract has been carried out and no issues were found.

However, depositing funds into a smart contract is always risky, as there may be bugs that went unnoticed during the audit. Never deposit money that you cannot afford to lose.

Whether you want to trade BEP-20 tokens, earn passive income with BAKE staking, or create special NFT Combo, BakerySwap offers you a ton of options.

Chapter 9

5 BSC Parameters to Keep an Eye On

We have talked about how public block-chains are permissionless, meaning that anyone with an address can interact with it. A less discussed feature is the fact that blockchain development is also permissionless. Anyone with the relevant skills can launch their dApp on a blockchain, and no one can stop it.

This leads to rapid development in the field of decentralized finance. Binance Smart Chain is only a few months old, but it is already seeing significant growth. There is a large amount of on-chain data available to the public, so it's easy for traders and investors to scrutinize the network's activity.

BscScan was developed by the same team that created EtherScan. It is a blockchain explorer and analytics platform for Binance Smart Chain, but it also has many other useful features. These can be great sources of information if you want to keep an eye on the DeFi on BSC.

In this chapter we take a look at five interesting parameter you should keep an eye on.

Yield farms on Binance Smart Chain

Yield farming is a way to generate crypto with your existing funds. Using platforms like PancakeSwap, you can generate returns on the Binance Smart Chain. As we will see with the next parameter, the commissions on BSC are extremely low. This makes the network ideal for smaller participants who want to enter the yield farming scene and reap some of the gains offered by the tools available.

The BscScan yield farming dashboard shows you all the current opportunities in this area. You can quickly access the latest farms and see information on what they do and how they work on dedicated websites. This should be the easiest bookmark ever if you are one of BSC's hard working farmers.

Another great resource for monitoring all the various dApps in the BSC ecosystem is https://mathdapp.store/. Just select Binance Smart Chain from the left menu and you will get a list of trusted dApps on BSC.

The average price of gas on the Binance Smart Chain

As we have mentioned in previous chapters, BSC has extremely low fees. On BSC, 1 gwei corresponds to 0.000000001 BNB.

With an average gas price of 20 gwei, sending 10 BNB equivalent to about $300 should cost around $0.01. Sending ten or even times that much shouldn't cost you more than a few cents. From the transaction history, we can see that some trades have paid higher fees. Some users may have reverted to their old habits on Ethereum or other compatible tools. It is not necessary. Binance Smart Chain is a long way from congestion, so 20 gwei should be enough.

The number of unique addresses on the Binance Smart Chain

BSC is cheap, but how can we roughly estimate how many users are on the blockchain? The number of unique addresses is a great way to start.

Does this mean that if a 100 unique address blockchain must have 100 unique users? Absolutely not. Anyone can create multiple addresses. And in any case, it would be rather difficult to find out if these addresses belong to the same entity.

So, we know that anyone can create multiple addresses, and this parameter is an overestimate. However, the number of unique addresses can give us a rough idea of the growth of the network.

Best BEP-20 Tokens

The Token Tracker page allows you to track the best BEP-20 tokens in terms of market capitalization or daily trading volume. This gives an idea of which tokens have the highest overall value on BSC, and which ones are experiencing the highest trading volumes.

One thing to keep in mind in this case is the token information. Those who manage tokens / smart contracts can update the information available on BscScan to provide more details regarding the token. If the token is not verified by the BscScan team, it may not be trusted.

You will see a lot of wrapped tokens on this page. For example, Binance-Peg ChainLink (LINK), i.e. LINK ERC-20 tokenized as BEP-20 token on BSC. What does wrapped mean? These assets are tokenized versions of a coin or token that belongs to another blockchain. This system allows you to use coins and tokens that are not present on BSC in Binance's DeFi ecosystem. For example, if you own LINK and want to use your tokens in yield farming on BSC, you can do so without selling them.

If you want to experiment with wrapped tokens, we encourage you to check out the Binance Bridge Project. Remember that while tokenizing a coin is a relatively easy process, it's not always necessary. You can simply exchange wrapped tokens that have already been tokenized by other people without worrying about the wrapping process.

Binance Smart Chain validators

To put it simply, validators are the participants who guarantee the BSC operation. Through BNB staking, they process transactions and confirm new blocks. In exchange for their services, they earn transaction fees from their network activity.

Binance Smart Chain is based on a consensus mechanism called Proof of Staked Authority. This consensus model can support minimal block time and low fees. You can see the main Binance Smart Chain validators by visiting the Validators Leaderboard.

Virtually anyone can become a validator, but the requirements are relatively high. After all, network security is at stake.

Whether you are a DeFi veteran or a complete beginner to yield farming on BSC, these metrics can help you improve your strategy for monitoring activity on Binance Smart Chain.

However, remember that markets are irrational, unpredictable and prone to periods of extreme volatility. Conducting your own research is critical to success in trading or yield farming. Among other steps to take, you can check if a token is verified by the BscScan team. If the smart contract is open source and has been checked, then you can visit the project's blog or social media accounts to learn more about it. Make sure you understand the risks associated with participating in DeFi before you risk your capital.

Facebook Libra (DIEM)

Libra (renamed Diem) is a payment system proposed by Facebook. It is based on a permissioned blockchain intended to support an ecosystem for digital payments and other financial services.

Its currency, called Diem (originally known as Libra), will be backed by a basket of stablecoins and is scheduled to launch in 2021. But what else do you need to know about Facebook's cryptocurrency? Let's find out together in this chapter.

Digital payments are an industry with many opportunities. More and more people have access to the internet via smartphones, and much of the economic activity takes place online. Companies like

PayPal, Visa and MasterCard already handle a lot of this business. Furthermore, many projects in the crypto sector are trying to build products for this sector.

However, unlike other projects, Facebook already has a large user base. Well, big might be an understatement. In the third quarter of 2020, Facebook had approximately 2.7 billion monthly active users. This could potentially make their payment system an instant hit.

What is Facebook Libra (Diem)?

Libra (renamed Diem) is a blockchain-based payment system proposed by Facebook in 2019. Its goal is to provide access to financial services for people without a bank account. Founding members include Morgan Beller, David Marcus and Kevin Weil.

The launch was originally scheduled for 2020, but has been postponed for various reasons and will likely take place in 2021.

Libra will be governed by the Libra Association (renamed the Diem Association), an independent association based in Geneva, Switzerland. The members of the association are various companies from the blockchain, tech, payments, telecommunications, venture capital and non-profit sectors.

Libra Association members are responsible for governance decisions, overseeing the operations of the Libra payment system and the projects developed on the Libra blockchain. Facebook aims to have 100 members in this association before the launch of Libra.

Is Libra a cryptocurrency?

Well, Libra is based on a blockchain, and it uses cryptographic technology. However, the term cryptocurrency usually implies specific properties that Libra does not possess. In short, it would be more correct to call Libra a digital currency.

How will Facebook Libra work?

The Libra Blockchain (renamed Diem Blockchain) is a permissioned blockchain that forms the backbone of this payment system. But what distinguishes it from other blockchains?

We have talked about permissionless blockchains such as those of Bitcoin or Ethereum. This means that anyone with an internet connection can freely access them, transact or develop on them. There is nothing and no one controlling access.

However, in the case of a permissioned blockchain the situation is quite different. To use it, you need permission from whoever is controlling the network. More precisely, the applications you use will need to have special access.

The fact that Libra is a permissioned blockchain also means that it doesn't use mining or staking to validate transactions like many other blockchains. Instead, it will rely on a group of authorized validators to validate transactions. These validators are the members of the Libra Association.

According to its creators, after the first five years Libra could turn into a Proof of Stake system. However, this is a very long time in such a nascent industry. So why not use PoS right from the start? Libra's white paper explains the reasons behind this decision. In their view, there is currently no permissionless system that can support the business of billions of people.

Is Facebook Libra decentralized or centralized?

According to many in the blockchain industry, permissioned blockchains cannot have the same degree of decentralization as their permissionless counterparts, as they are more like a traditional corporate database.

In this sense, Libra is not as resistant to censorship as Bitcoin and other cryptocurrencies. Since these validators must be members of the Libra Association, the network could end up being relatively centralized. On the other hand, controlling and verifying which applications can interact with the distributed ledger can have its advantages. For example, it may be easier to rule out malicious applications and scams.

The Libra payment system

Libra payment system supports several single currency stablecoins pegged to fiat currencies, such as USD, EUR, GBP. These work in a similar way to the stablecoins you may already know, in that their value is derived from a reserve called the Libra Reserve. This reserve consists of cash, cash equivalents and short-term government bonds.

Additionally, the Libra payment system will also support a multi-currency coin called Diem Dollar (ticker symbol LBR). It is a sort of a combination of all the other stablecoins in the system, and is backed by a basket of assets that ensures its value. You can think of it as a stablecoin of stablecoins. The idea is that these various forms of collateral can protect users from volatility. This is an important aspect for something that aims to act as a form of payment.

The Libra cryptocurrency can be stored in an incoming wallet called Novi (formerly Calibra Wallet). As expected, this digital wallet could be integrated into other social media products, such as Facebook Messenger and WhatsApp. According to the plans, users should be able to easily convert between US dollars (or other fiat currencies) and Facebook's currency.

Libra's source code, called Diem Core, is open source and written in Rust. Everyone can see the code directly on Diem's GitHub page. According to plans, Libra will also support smart contract functionality through a programming language called Move.

Facebook Libra and Bitcoin

At this point, it is evident that Libra and Bitcoin are fundamentally different and may very well coexist in the future. While both can be considered digital payment systems, they aim to serve different use cases.

Bitcoin is a decentralized and censorship-resistant cryptocurrency that often serves as a reserve asset or store of value. Libra, on the other hand, is a proposal based on a permissioned network that suggests a more centralized model.

The future of Libra

Facebook has received several criticisms following the original Libra announcement, mostly from central banks, lawmakers and regulators. It remains to be seen whether they will manage to combine all the elements necessary to make Libra a successful project.

We are excited about Libra and we look forward to using it. Of course, since its price is going to be stable, you cannot consider it an investment.

Chapter 11

Bitcoin ETF

Bitcoin and the cryptocurrency market have come a long way. A decade ago, this technology was only used by a small community of enthusiasts. In this period the price was around 10,000 BTC for two pizzas.

In just a few years we have seen several successful companies make their way in this sector, we have seen the development of many new cryptocurrencies, the birth of DeFi and much more. On top of all this, institutional adoption is also growing. MicroStrategy has converted more than $2 billion of its balance sheet into Bitcoin and you may soon be able to buy the latest Tesla model with your BTC.

What key steps are missing before Bitcoin can become an important asset in the global macroeconomic environment? One of these could be a regulated instrument that allows traditional institutions and traders to gain exposure to BTC. According to some, the best way would be via an ETF.

What is a Bitcoin ETF?

Let's start from the definition. An ETF is an exchange traded fund, which is an investment fund that tracks the price of an underlying asset. ETFs are used in various sectors and for different types of assets. For example, gold ETFs have been around for decades and track its price.

A Bitcoin ETF would work the same way. The ETF's price would follow Bitcoin's.

ETFs are regulated financial products, which are traded on traditional markets such as the NASDAQ or NYSE and not on a cryptocurrency exchange. This situation could change in the future, as the boundaries between traditional finance and the cryptocurrency industry are getting closer and closer.

The importance of a Bitcoin ETF

Bitcoin is not the easiest asset to manage. For example, custody can cause major headaches for a large institution. After all, Goldman Sachs won't just link a hardware wallet to a PC and "YOLO" $ 2billion in Bitcoin. Large financial institutions do not operate in the same way as individual investors; they need a complex regulatory framework flanked by a financial system to be able to move in this sector.

This is why an ETF can make a difference in broadening adoption and potential investor base. It could offer exposure to traders in traditional markets, without the latter having to worry about everything needed to physically own the coins.

A Bitcoin ETF could also contain other assets besides BTC. For example, a Bitcoin ETF could contain a basket of other assets such as Bitcoin, Ethereum, Tesla shares, gold, and so on. This would lead to diversification useful for investors.

A brief overview of Bitcoin ETFs

Generally, when we talk about Bitcoin ETFs, we usually talk about ETFs on US markets. However, ETFs exist in many other markets. For example, the first Bitcoin ETF was launched on the Canadian stock market. It is called the Purpose Bitcoin ETF and is traded on the Toronto Stock Exchange under the BTCC ticker.

The focus is currently on US regulators, as the US financial market is the largest in the world. A US Bitcoin ETF could consolidate Bitcoin as an investment asset.

There have been several attempts to launch a Bitcoin ETF in the United States. As of March 2021, they have all been rejected by the US Securities and Exchange Commission (SEC).

Why does the SEC keep rejecting such regulatory requests? These are the arguments for denying the claims of a Bitcoin ETF: the volatility, the unregulated nature of the Bitcoin markets and the apparent vulnerability of the latter to market manipulation. While these arguments may be plausible to some extent, the fact remains that the same could be true for many other financial markets that already have an ETF.

Furthermore, much of the financial structure required to legitimize Bitcoin as a macro asset class was built during the last bear market. If MicroStrategy, just a few years ago, had wanted to buy billions of dollars in Bitcoin, it probably would have been very difficult. Now, both the infrastructure and the liquidity are mature enough to be able to manage even such substantial investments.

Probably, the continuous evolution of the Bitcoin market will change the cards on the table for the regulatory bodies, so as to lead to the possible birth of a US Bitcoin ETF. It's hard to say when it will happen but it may be sooner than we think.

Should you invest in a Bitcoin ETF?

Is a Bitcoin ETF the right financial tool to invest in Bitcoin? Well, if your intention is to protect your savings from devaluing fiat currencies, it might be best to buy Bitcoin directly.

After all, Bitcoin is democratized finance. Having direct custody of your savings can be very useful. Not to mention the countless ways you can earn an annuity or borrow, using your Bitcoins as collateral.
That said, there are also advantages to a Bitcoin ETF, if you find them interesting, in this case an ETF can also be a good choice.

A Bitcoin ETF allows traditional market investors to gain exposure to Bitcoin in a regulated manner. It can be a good way to achieve more institutional adoption of the crypto world as an asset class. When will US regulators agree to issue a Bitcoin ETF in the US? It is difficult to say, but it seems that all the pieces are falling into place.
We will not invest in a Bitcoin ETF, because we believe that it is much better to own your BTC directly.

Chapter 12

Earning with Crypto: Staking

In the next few chapters we are going to talk about some of the methods cryptocurrency offer to earn passive income on your investments. We strongly believe that a good crypto portfolio has a part dedicated to dividend yielding, especially now that standard interest rates are near 0.

You can think of staking as an alternative to mining that requires the use of fewer resources. It involves holding funds in a cryptocurrency wallet to support the security and operations of a blockchain network.

Simply put, staking is the act of blocking cryptocurrencies to receive rewards.

In most cases, you will be able to stake your coins directly from your crypto wallet, such as Trust Wallet or MetaMask. Additionally, many exchanges offer staking services to their users. Binance Staking, for instance, allows you to earn rewards in an extremely simple way. In fact, all you have to do is keep your coins on the exchange. This is another reason why we love Binance so much.

To better understand staking, you will first need to understand how Proof of Stake works. PoS is a consensus mechanism that allows blockchains to operate with greater energy efficiency while maintaining a decent degree of decentralization

A look at PoS

Proof of Work has proven to be a very robust mechanism for facilitating consensus in a decentralized context. However, the problem is that it involves a great deal of arbitrary computation. The puzzle that miners compete to solve has no other purpose than to keep the network secure. It could be argued that this in itself makes over-computation justifiable. At this point, you may be wondering: are there no other ways to maintain decentralized consensus without the high computational cost?

Proof of Stake is the answer to this question. The central idea is that participants can block coins, and at particular intervals, the protocol will randomly assign one of them the right to validate the next block. Typically, the likelihood of being chosen is proportional to the amount of coins. This means that the more coins you block, the higher your odds.

In this way, what determines which participants create a block is not based on their ability to solve hash problems like in Proof of Work. Instead, it is determined by how many coins they hold in staking.

Some might argue that block production through staking allows for a greater degree of scalability for blockchains. This is one of the reasons why the Ethereum network has planned a migration from PoW to PoS in a set of technical updates collectively known as ETH 2.0.

The inventor of Proof of Stake

One of the first Proof of Stake appearances can be attributed to Sunny King and Scott Nadal in their 2012 paper for Peercoin. They describe it as a "peer-to-peer cryptocurrency design derived from Satoshi Nakamoto's Bitcoin."

The Peercoin network was launched with a hybrid PoW / PoS mechanism, where the PoW was mainly used to issue the initial supply. However, it was not necessary for the long-term sustainability of the network, and its importance was gradually reduced. In fact, much of the network's security was based on PoS.

Delegated Proof of Stake

An alternative version of this mechanism was developed in 2014 by Daniel Larimer called Delegated Proof of Stake or DPoS. It was first used as part of the BitShares blockchain, but shortly after other networks adopted the model. These include Steem and EOS, also created by Larimer.

DPoS allows users to commit their balances as votes, where the voting power is proportional to the number of coins in their possession. These votes are then used to elect a number of delegates who run the blockchain on behalf of their constituents, ensuring security and consensus. Typically, staking rewards are distributed to these elected delegates, who distribute part of the rewards to their constituents in proportion to their individual contributions.

The DPoS model allows consensus to be achieved with fewer validation nodes. Because of this, it tends to improve network performance. On the other hand, it can also result in a lesser degree of decentralization as the network relies on a small select group of validation nodes. These nodes manage the operations and the governance of the blockchain. They participate in the processes to reach consensus and define fundamental governance parameters.

In other words, DPoS allows users to report their influence through other network participants.

How staking works

As we have already discussed before, Proof of Work systems rely on mining to add new blocks to the blockchain. On the contrary, Proof of Stake networks produce and validate new blocks through the staking process. Staking consists in the freezing of coins by validators in order to be randomly selected by the protocol at specific intervals to create a block. Usually, participants who stake a larger stake have a higher chance of being chosen as the next block validator.

This allows you to produce blocks without relying on specialized mining hardware, such as ASICs. While ASIC mining requires a significant investment in hardware, staking requires a direct investment in the cryptocurrency itself. Therefore, instead of competing for the next block with computational work, PoS validators are selected based on the number of coins they are staking with. The "stake" is what motivates validators to maintain network security. If they don't, their entire stakes could be at risk.

While each Proof of Stake blockchain has its own particular staking currency, some networks adopt a two-token system where rewards are distributed using the second token.

On a very practical level, staking simply means holding funds in a suitable wallet. This allows anyone to perform various functions for the network in exchange for staking rewards.

Calculating staking rewards

Each blockchain network can use a different way to calculate staking rewards.

Some methods are regulated on a block-by-block basis, taking several factors into consideration. These can include:

- how many coins the validator has in staking
- how long the validator has been actively staking
- how many coins are staking on the network in total
- the rate of inflation

However, for some networks staking rewards are determined as a fixed percentage. These rewards are distributed to validators as a kind of inflation compensation, which encourages users to spend their coins instead of keeping them, potentially increasing their use as cryptocurrencies.

A predictable rewards program can be beneficial for someone. Furthermore, considering that the reward percentage is made public, it could incentivize more participants to take part in the staking process.

Staking pools

A staking pool is a group of coin holders who pool their resources to increase the odds of validating blocks and receiving rewards. They combine their staking power and share rewards proportionally to individual contributions to the pool.

Creating and maintaining a staking pool often takes a lot of time and expertise. Staking pools tend to be most effective on networks where the barriers to entry are relatively high. For this reason, many pool providers charge a commission on the staking rewards distributed to participants.

Additionally, pools can provide greater flexibility to individual stakers. Typically, the stake must be locked for a fixed period and usually has a withdrawal or dissolution period set by the protocol. Furthermore, a substantial minimum balance is almost always required for staking, with the aim of discouraging malicious behavior.

Most staking pools require a low minimum balance and do not impose additional withdrawal times. Therefore, joining a staking pool instead of staking alone might be ideal for new users.

Cold staking

Cold staking refers to the staking process on a wallet that is not connected to the internet. This can be done using a hardware wallet, but it is also possible with an air-gapped software wallet.

Networks that support cold staking allow users to stake while securely storing their funds offline. It is important to note that if the owner moves their coins out of cold storage, they will no longer receive the rewards.

Cold staking is particularly useful for large holders who want to ensure maximum protection of their funds and support the network at the same time.

Our favorite coins to stake are KAVA, ADA and BNB. Once ETH 2.0 will be released, we will stake our ETH as well.

Chapter 13

Yield Farming

The second method you can use to earn passive income on your cryptocurrency is called Yield Farming and in this chapter we are going to tell you everything you need to know about it.

The decentralized finance movement has been at the forefront of innovation in the blockchain industry. DeFi applications are permissionless, so anyone with an internet connection and a supported wallet can interact with them. Furthermore, they usually do not require trust in any third party. In other words, they are trustless.

One of the new concepts that emerged from this area is yield farming. This is a new way to earn rewards using cryptocurrency funds through permissionless liquidity protocols. It allows anyone to generate passive income using the decentralized ecosystem built on Ethereum. For this reason, yield farming may change the way investors hold their coins in the future.

What yield farming is

Yield farming, also known as liquidity mining, is a way to make money using cryptocurrency funds. Simply put, it means blocking cryptocurrencies to receive rewards.

From a certain point of view, yield farming can be compared to staking. However, there is much more complexity in the background. In many cases, it involves users called liquidity providers (LPs) who add funds to liquidity pools.

A liquidity pool is a smart contract that contains funds. In exchange for the liquidity provided to the pool, liquidity providers receive a reward, which can be composed of commissions generated by the underlying DeFi platform or from other sources.

Some liquidity pools distribute the rewards in different tokens, which can be deposited into other liquidity pools to earn from there as well, and so on. You can already imagine how incredibly complex strategies can emerge. However, the basic idea is that a liquidity provider deposits funds into a liquidity pool and receives rewards in return.

Yield farming usually takes place on Ethereum with ERC-20 tokens, and rewards are paid in an ERC-20 token. However, this may change in the future. Why? Because in the future cross-chain bridges and other similar advances could allow DeFi applications to become independent of a particular blockchain. This means they could run on other blockchains that support smart contract functionality.

Typically, yield farmers often shift their funds from one protocol to another in search of high yields. As a result, DeFi platforms could provide other economic incentives to attract more capital as well. As with centralized exchanges, liquidity tends to attract more liquidity.

What triggered the yield farming boom?

The sudden and strong interest in yield farming can be attributed to the launch of COMP, the governance token of the Compound Finance ecosystem. Tokens of this type confer governance rights to the holders. But how to distribute these tokens to make the network as decentralized as possible? Well, a common way to start a decentralized blockchain is to distribute these governance tokens algorithmically, with liquidity incentives. This represents an incentive for liquidity providers to "farm" the new token by providing liquidity to the protocol.

While it didn't invent yield farming, the launch of COMP gave a big boost to this token distribution model. Since then, other DeFi projects have come up with innovative schemes to attract liquidity to their ecosystems.

The Total Blocked Value (TVL)

The Total Blocked Value (TVL) is a metric that measures how many cryptocurrencies are stuck in loans and other types of DeFi money markets.

In a sense, TVL represents aggregate liquidity in liquidity pools. It is a useful index for measuring the health of DeFi and the yield farming market as a whole. Furthermore, it is an effective benchmark for comparing the "market share" of the different DeFi protocols.

To monitor the TVL we can use Defi Pulse. On Defi Pulse you can see which platforms have the most ETH or other crypto assets locked in DeFi. This should give you a general idea of the current state of yield farming. Of course, the greater the locked-in value, the greater the ongoing yield farming activity. It is worth noting that it is possible to measure TVL in ETH, USD or even BTC. Each will offer a different perspective on DeFi's money market conditions.

How yield farming works

Yield farming is closely tied to a model called the automated market maker or AMM.

Liquidity providers deposit funds into a liquidity pool. This pool is used by a marketplace where users can lend, borrow, or trade tokens. Using these platforms incurs fees, which are then distributed to liquidity providers based on their share of the liquidity pool. This is the basic structure of how an automated market maker works.

However, the implementations can be very different. We should never forget that it is a new technology. We will certainly see the launch of new approaches that bring improvements to current implementations.

In addition to fees, another incentive to add funds to a liquidity pool could be the distribution of a new token. For example, a project could create a system where the only way to receive its token is by providing liquidity to a specific pool, as this is not available in the open market.

The rules of distribution depend entirely on the implementation of the protocol. The key point is that liquidity providers receive a reward based on the amount of liquidity they provide to the pool.

Deposited funds are usually USD-pegged stablecoins. However, this is not a strict requirement. Among the most popular stablecoins in DeFi we find DAI, USDT, USDC, and BUSD. Some protocols issue tokens that represent the coins deposited in the system. For example, if you deposit DAI in Compound, you will receive cDAI, or Compound DAI. If you deposit ETH in Compound, you will receive cETH.

As you can imagine, there can be different levels of complexity in this context. You could deposit your cDAIs in another protocol that issues a third token to represent your cDAIs, which in turn represent your DAIs and so on. These chains can become very complex and difficult to follow. We will not get into the more complex yield farming strategies, as we do not use them.

Calculating yield farming yields

Typically, yields from yield farming are calculated on an annual basis. The estimates thus obtained represent profits generated over a year.

Some commonly used parameters are the annual percentage rate (APR) and the annual percentage yield (APY). The difference between the two is that the APR does not consider the effects of compounding, while the APY does. Compounding, in this case, indicates the process of directly reinvesting profits to generate more returns. However, be aware that in some cases APR and APY may be used interchangeably.

It should also be remembered that we are only talking about estimates and projections. The actual rewards are quite difficult to accurately estimate. In fact, yield farming is a highly competitive and fast-paced market, and the rewards can fluctuate quickly. If a yield farming strategy works for a while, several farmers will take advantage of the opportunity, and the returns obtained from it will be lower.

Since APR and APY derive from traditional markets, DeFi may have to find its own parameters to calculate returns. Due to the fast pace of the industry, it may be more useful to estimate weekly or even daily returns.

DeFi and collateralization

Typically, you need to provide collateral to borrow assets. Basically it acts as insurance for your loan. Depending on which protocol you decide to provide funds to, you may need to keep an eye on collateralization.

If the value of your collateral falls below the limit required by the protocol, it could be liquidated on the open market. To avoid this scenario, you can add more collateral.

Each platform has a particular set of rules for this process and a different collateralization ratio required. Furthermore, on most of these platforms we find a concept called "overcollateralization". This means that borrowers have to deposit more value than they want to borrow, to reduce the liquidation risk following violent market crashes.

For instance, suppose the loan protocol you want to use requires a collateralization ratio of 200%. This means that for every $100 of value you provide, you can borrow $50. However, it is usually safer to add more collateral than required to further reduce the liquidation risk. That said, several systems use high collateralisation ratios to keep the entire platform relatively safe from liquidation risk. The collateral can even reach 750% of the borrowed amount.

Risks of yield farming

As you can imagine, yield farming isn't easy. The most profitable strategies are extremely complex and indicated only for expert users. Additionally, yield farming is generally more suitable for those with a lot of capital to invest.

This practice is not as simple as it sounds, and if you don't understand what you are doing you will probably end up losing money. We talked about the liquidation danger on your collateral, but there are risks you need to know before getting started with yield farming.

An obvious risk of yield farming involves smart contracts. Given the nature of DeFi, many protocols are created and developed by small teams with limited budgets. This can increase the risk of bugs in smart contracts.

Even in the case of larger protocols verified by reputable auditors, new bugs and vulnerabilities are often found. Due to the immutable nature of the blockchain, this can lead to a loss of user funds. Take this into account when blocking your funds in a smart contract.

Furthermore, one of the main advantages of DeFi is also one of its greatest risks: the concept of composability. Let's examine its impact on yield farming.

As already mentioned, DeFi protocols are permissionless and can be easily integrated with each other, so the entire DeFi ecosystem is heavily dependent on each of its building blocks. This is what we mean when we say such applications are composable. They can work together easily.

The problem arises when one of the elements doesn't work as expected, and the entire ecosystem suffers. This is one of the biggest risks for yield farmers and liquidity pools. Not only do you have to trust the protocol you deposit your funds into, but also all the others that that protocol depends on.

Yield farming platforms and protocols

What is the best way to make money with yield farming? This question has no definitive answer. Yield farming strategies can change in a matter of hours. Each platform and strategy has its own set of rules and risks. If you want to get started with yield farming, you first need to familiarize yourself with how decentralized liquidity protocols work.

You already know the basic idea. Deposit funds into a smart contract and receive rewards in return. However, implementations can vary widely, so it's generally not a good idea to blindly deposit your funds and hope for high returns. As a basic rule of risk management, you need to be able to stay in control of your investment.

That being said, let's take a look at some of the protocols that form the core of yield farming strategies.

Compound Finance

Compound is an algorithmic money market that allows users to lend and borrow assets. Anyone with an Ethereum wallet can provide assets to Compound's liquidity pool and earn rewards that immediately begin producing compound interest. Rates are adjusted algorithmically based on supply and demand. Compound is one of the central protocols in the yield farming ecosystem.

MakerDAO

Maker is a decentralized credit platform that supports the creation of DAI, an algorithmically anchored stablecoin to the value of the USD. Anyone can open a

Maker Vault to freeze collateral, such as ETH, BAT, USDC, or WBTC, generating DAI as debt against the blocked collateral. This debt accrues interest over time, called the stability fee. The rate of this fee is set by holders of MKR tokens.

Yield farmers can use Maker to issue DAI for use in yield farming strategies.

Synthetix

Synthetix is a protocol for synthetic assets. It allows the stake of Synthetix Network Token (SNX) or ETH as collateral against which to issue synthetic assets. Virtually anything that has a reliable price feed can be a synthetic asset. Therefore, any financial asset can be added to the Synthetix platform.

In the future, Synthetix could allow all sorts of assets to be used for yield farming. Do you want to use long-term gold investments in a yield farming strategy? Synthetic assets may be the solution.

Aave

Aave is a decentralized lending and borrowing protocol. Interest rates are adjusted algorithmically, based on market conditions. Creditors receive "aToken" in exchange for their funds. Upon deposit, these tokens immediately begin to accrue compound interest. Additionally, Aave offers other more advanced features, including flash loans.

As a decentralized lending protocol, Aave is widely used by yield farmers.

Uniswap

Uniswap is a decentralized exchange protocol that allows token exchanges in a trustless system. Liquidity providers deposit an equivalent value of two tokens to create a market. After that, traders can trade using this liquidity pool. As a reward for their service, liquidity providers earn commissions from the trades that take place in their pool.

Uniswap is one of the most popular platforms for trustless token swaps due to its user friendly nature. It can be a useful tool for yield farming strategies.

Curve Finance

Curve Finance is a decentralized exchange protocol designed specifically for efficient stablecoin swaps. Unlike other similar protocols like Uniswap, Curve allows users to swap large amounts of stablecoins with relatively low slippage.

As you can imagine, given the abundance of stablecoins in the yield farming landscape, Curve pools are a key part of the DeFi infrastructure.

Balancer

Balancer is a liquidity protocol similar to Uniswap and Curve. However, the key difference is that it offers custom token allocations in a liquidity pool. As a result, liquidity providers can create custom Balancer pools instead of following Uniswap's 50/50 allocation. Just like the latter, LPs earn commissions for transactions made in their liquidity pools.

Thanks to the flexibility it introduces in the creation of pools, Balancer is an important innovation for yield farming strategies.

Yearn.finance

Yearn.finance is a decentralized ecosystem of aggregators for loan services such as Aave, Compound and others. Its goal is to optimize token lending by algorithmically finding the most profitable services. After deposit, funds are converted into yTokens which rebalance periodically to maximize profits.

Yearn.finance is a useful tool for farmers looking for a protocol that automatically chooses the best strategies for them.
We absolutely love Yearn.finance and it is the main service we use to do yield farming.

Conclusion

Congratulations on making it to the end of this book, we hope you found some useful insights to take your cryptocurrency trading skills to the next level. As you should know by now, the world of cryptocurrency is extremely complicated and there is a new "opportunity" every way you look. However, our experience tells us that only by taking things seriously and having a proper plan you can develop your investing skills to the point that you can actually accumulate wealth.

Our final advice is to stay away from the shining objects that the world of cryptocurrencies offers you every day. Simply study the world of cryptocurrencies in depth and when you feel ready try to invest a little bit of money. Analyze your results, improve your money management skills and become the master of your emotions.

As you can see, there are no shortcuts you can take. Easy money does not exist. What exists is the possibility to start from zero and work your way up to become a professional cryptocurrency investor. The journey might be difficult, but it is certainly worth it.

To your success!

Bitcoin, Cryptocurrency, NFT and DeFi

Create Generational Wealth During the 2021 Bull Run and Learn How to Take Advantage of the Life Changing Opportunities provided by the Blockchain!

by Barry Johnson

The following Book is reproduced below with the goal of providing information that is as accurate and reliable as possible. Regardless, purchasing this Book can be seen as consent to the fact that both the publisher and the author of this book are in no way experts on the topics discussed within and that any recommendations or suggestions that are made herein are for entertainment purposes only. Professionals should be consulted as needed prior to undertaking any of the action endorsed herein. This declaration is deemed fair and valid by both the American Bar Association and the Committee of Publishers Association and is legally binding throughout the United States. Furthermore, the transmission, duplication, or reproduction of any of the following work including specific information will be considered an illegal act irrespective of if it is done electronically or in print. This extends to creating a secondary or tertiary copy of the work or a recorded copy and is only allowed with the express written consent from the Publisher. All additional rights reserved. The information in the following pages is broadly considered a truthful and accurate account of facts and as such, any inattention, use, or misuse of the information in question by

the reader will render any resulting actions solely under their purview. There are no scenarios in which the publisher or the original author of this work can be in any fashion deemed liable for any hardship or damages that may befall them after undertaking information described herein.

Additionally, the information in the following pages is intended only for informational purposes and should thus be thought of as universal. As befitting its nature, it is presented without assurance regarding its prolonged validity or interim quality. Trademarks that are mentioned are done without written consent and can in no way be considered an endorsement from the trademark holder.

Table of Contents

Introduction

itcoin has taken the world by storm once again when it crossed $20,000 per BTC in December of last year. After more than 2 years of bear market, the most famous cryptocurrency surpassed its previous all time high.

A lot of people are now trying to improvise themselves as professional investors and are losing a lot of money, only helping those who actually know what they are doing accumulate an incredible amount of wealth that will lead to generational fortunes.

To join the club of the few investors that actually make it, you need the right knowledge and the right mindset. Notice how we did not include a large initial capital. In fact, while having more money to invest means having more fire power, it is not necessary to have thousands of dollars to accumulate cryptocurrency and build wealth.

In fact, when we started investing in cryptocurrency we only had a few hundreds to put into the market, but that sum yielded us thousands and thousands of dollars over the span of a few years.

In this book you are going to discover everything there is to know about the fascinating world of cryptocurrency. From the operation of the Bitcoin blockchain to more advanced projects, like Uniswap and Compound.
If you diligently study the content of this book, we are sure you are going to see take your crypto knowledge to the next level. This also means you are going to see amazing results in a relative short period of time, since this bull run is offering an amazing number of opportunities.

To your success!

Barry Johnson

Chapter 1

Curve Finance (CRV)

In the previous chapter, we mentioned the Curve Finance protocol. Since it plays a fundamental role when it comes to DeFi, we believe it is important to dive a bit deeper into what it is and how it works.

Automated Market Makers have had a major impact on the crypto landscape. Liquidity protocols like Uniswap, Balancer and PancakeSwap allow anyone to become a market maker and earn commissions on many currency pairs.

Can these AMMs significantly compete with centralized exchanges? Maybe. But there is one sector of the market where they are already showing great potential and that is stablecoin trading. Curve Finance is at the forefront in this context.

What Curve Finance is

Curve Finance is an automated market maker protocol designed for trading between stablecoins with minimal fees and slippage. It is a decentralized liquidity aggregator where anyone can add assets to different liquidity pools and earn commissions.

Because of the way the pricing formula works on Curve, it can also be extremely useful for trading tokens that trade in a relatively small price range.
This means that they are not only valid for exchanges between stablecoins, but also between different tokenized versions of a coin. Hence, Curve is one of the best ways to trade different tokenized versions of Bitcoin, such as WBTC, renBTC, and sBTC.

At the time of writing, Curve is making 36 pools available to trade different stablecoins and assets. Of course, these are constantly changing based on market demand and DeFi's ever-changing landscape. Some of the more popular stablecoins available include USDT, USDC, DAI, BUSD, TUSD, and sUSD.

There is no official information relating to the Curve team, but most of the contributions on GitHub were made by Michael Egorov, the CTO of a cybersecurity company called NuCypher.

How Curve Finance works

As already mentioned, assets are priced based on a certain formula instead of an order book. The formula used by Curve is specially designed to facilitate trades that occur in an approximately similar range.

For example, we know that 1 USDT should equal 1 USDC, which in turn equals 1 BUSD, and so on. However, if you want to convert $100 million USDT to USDC, and then convert it to BUSD, you will have to contend with some slippage. Curve's formula is designed to minimize this slippage as much as possible.

One thing to take into consideration is that if these assets weren't in the same price range, the Curve formula would not work efficiently. However, the system does not take this possibility into account. After all, if USDT is worth $0.7, something else outside of Curve has gone terribly wrong. The system cannot solve things outside its control, so as long as the tokens hold their value, the formula does its job very well.

This results in extremely low slippage even for large trades. In fact, the spread on Curve can hold its own against some centralized exchanges and OTC trading desks with the best liquidity.

There are several assumptions about trust and risk, so liquidity and execution are not the full picture. However, it is undoubtedly exciting to see the competition between the centralized and the decentralized world.

The CRV token

CRV is the governance token of CurveDAO, a decentralized autonomous organization that manages the protocol. CRV is constantly distributed to the liquidity providers of the protocol, at a rate that decreases on an annual basis.

As of April 2021, each trade on the platform carries a 0.04% trading fee which is distributed directly to liquidity providers.

Risks of Curve Finance

Curve was verified by a company called Trail of Bits. However, this audit does not mean that the project is completely safe to use. When you use any smart contract, there are always risks, no matter how many audits have been done. Deposit only what you are willing to lose.

As with any other automated market maker protocol, you will need to consider impermanent loss as well.

Behind the scenes, the liquidity pool could also be provided to Compound or yearn.finance in order to generate greater income for liquidity providers. Furthermore, thanks to the magic of modularity, trading on Curve is not only reserved for users, but is available to other smart contracts as well. This introduces additional risks, as many of these DeFi protocols become dependent on each other. If one breaks, we could see a damaging chain reaction across the entire DeFi ecosystem.

Swerve Finance

Like SushiSwap and Uniswap, Curve Finance has a high profile hard fork as well. This hard fork is called Swerve Finance.

Swerve is advertised as a "fair launch," meaning that its governance token (SWRV) has not been distributed with an allocation reserved for the team or founder. SWRV tokens were distributed through a liquidity mining event, where everyone had an equal opportunity to farm them. Therefore, Swerve claims to be a 100% community-managed fork of Curve.

Curve is one of the most popular automated market makers active on Ethereum. It facilitates high-volume stablecoin trading with minimal slippage and tight spreads on a non-custodial basis.

Another feature that places Curve Finance at the heart of the DeFi industry is the fact that other blockchain protocols are highly dependent on its functions. Composability between different decentralized applications carries risks, but it is also one of the main advantages of DeFi.

When we want to go from one stablecoin to another, we always use Curve Finance, as slippage is basically non existent. We encourage you to check it out and familiarize with it before doing anything.

Chapter 2

Alpha Homora (ALPHA)

Yield farming in the DeFi sector often involves providing liquidity to a decentralized exchange such as Uniswap. In return, users can earn a portion of the commissions generated by the trading pair they are providing liquidity to.

Alpha Homora allows you to increase your yield farming position with up to 2.5x leverage. It also allows you to earn based on your personal preferences and risk appetite. This way, you can increase your overall returns from liquidity mining. However, using leverage also increases the associated risks. Let's see how this all works.

The most successful projects in DeFi allow users to participate in yield farming by providing liquidity.

Most of these initiatives are based on the Ethereum ecosystem. Binance Smart Chain also supports this type of functionality, which is why the Alpha Finance Lab team has decided to build its DeFi ecosystem on both BSC and Ethereum.

What is Alpha Homora?

Alpha Homora is the second working product developed by Alpha Finance Lab. It is designed to allow users to increase their exposure to liquidity mining. More precisely, those who participate in yield farming in DeFi can "amplify" their positions. This is probably the first case in which leverage enters the scene for yield farmers, making Alpha Homora a unique project in the decentralized finance landscape.

However, yield farming isn't the only option to explore. Alpha Homora supports ETH loans and allows participants to become special users called liquidators and bounty hunters. We'll see what they mean later on in this chapter. The essential point is that all of these options allow users to earn based on their personal preferences and their risk appetite. Such features provide high APY returns, making Alpha Homora attractive to DeFi enthusiasts.

Alpha Homora's options for yield farming

The first option to explore in Alpha Homora is yield farming. Once their wallet is connected, the user can deposit funds, set up leverage and start farming immediately.

At the moment, the pools supported by Alpha Homora include the following.

WETH / WBTC (Uniswap)
WETH / USDT (Uniswap)
WETH / USDC (Uniswap)
WETH / DAI (Uniswap)
WETH / DPI (IndexCoop)

A crucial aspect of yield farming via Alpha Homora is that every ALPHA token that is farmed is reinvested every day. According to the team, this offers higher profit potential in a completely passive way.

The ALPHA token explained

ALPHA is both a utility token and a governance token. It plays this role not only for the Alpha Homora protocol, but for other products in the Alpha Finance ecosystem as well. The ALPHA token is also the first project launched on both Binance Launchpad and Launchpool.
Use cases include providing liquidity, staking to receive a share of the protocol fees, and unlocking interoperability features between Alpha products.

In terms of governance, there are two aspects to consider. First of all, ALPHA token holders can manage key parameters of specific products, including interest rates, value ratios, liquidation penalties, and so on. The second point concerns the broader governance at the protocol level. According to Alpha

Finance Lab, in the future ALPHA holders will be able to determine how the different Alpha products can work together more seamlessly.

The advantages of Alpha Homora

Innovation

Alpha Homora introduces new ways to participate in yield farming. These are useful for both yield farmers and the DeFi sector in general. Alpha Homora allows users to earn higher APYs without having to trust any intermediary.

Security audit

Smart contract audits are a key issue for investors. Several DeFi projects were launched without a proper security audit. Instead, Alpha Homora's smart contracts have been vetted and verified by Peckshield. Peckshield is a trust resource in the audit space.

Governance token

The addition of Alpha Homora to the Alpha Finance ecosystem introduces an additional synergy for the ALPHA token. As with other Alpha products, tokens are used in the governance of the Alpha Homora protocol. Involving the community is an important step towards long-term sustainability.

The risks of Alpha Homora

Liquidation

Be very careful with any strategy that includes leverage. You should only deposit funds if you fully understand the liquidation risks. At Alpha Homora, yield farmers run the risk of being liquidated. As long as users remain above 80% creditworthiness for Uniswap and 60% for IndexCoop, the positions will not be liquidated. This means that a leveraged position can be liquidated on Uniswap when the debt is more than 80% of the position value. This does not take slippage into account, so you need to be even more careful.

Potential vulnerabilities

Remember, code auditing does not mean that using the smart contract is safe. Bugs and vulnerabilities will always be part of any software. You need to keep this in mind when interacting with any smart contract.

Ethereum vault

By using Alpha Homora, you can earn interest on your Ether through an interest-bearing position. You can deposit ETH in Alpha Homora Bank and receive ibETH tokens in exchange. These ibETH tokens are tradable assets that accumulate interest and represent your share of ETH in the Bank's pool.

The interest paid by the ETH borrower is distributed to the ETH lender, in proportion to their share of the pool. The interest rate is determined by the Bank's utilization rate. The higher this rate is, the higher the interest rate will be. Simply put, the higher the demand for loans, the higher the interest rate.

A portion of the interest paid is sent to a treasury that acts as an insurance fund to offer protection from black swan events.

Liquidators and bounty hunters

Alpha Homora's platform offers other unique features. Special users called liquidators can liquidate risky positions. This happens when a user's position value falls below the settlement ratio for the respective platform. Hence, positions below the liquidation threshold run the risk of being liquidated manually. The liquidator receives 5% of the liquidated value as a commission.

Bounty hunters are another type of special user. They can use a function in the smart contract that sells all tokens obtained through yield farming in Alpha Homora's portfolio, converting them to Ether. By doing so, the bounty hunters reinvest the ETH collected in the yield farming pool, receiving 3% of the total reward. This, in turn, reduces the amount of ibETH tokens earned by the lender, as their share in the pool decreases.

The launch of Alpha Homora is an important milestone for the Alpha Finance ecosystem. The ability to open leveraged positions on liquidity mining is a significant innovation for the DeFi industry in general.

While yield farming is the main selling point, its interest-bearing Ethereum accounts can be attractive to more experienced users. Combined with the ability to become a liquidator or bounty hunter, the blockchain community has many ways to interact with this platform.

We have invested in ALPHA back in December 2020 and we have no plan in selling our coins. However, we have never tried the protocol ourselves.

Chapter 3

Liquidity Pools

Liquidity pools are one of the core technologies behind the current DeFi ecosystem. They are an essential part of automated market makers, lending protocols, yield farming, synthetic assets, on-chain insurance, and blockchain video games.

In itself, the idea is really simple. A liquidity pool basically consists of funds put together in a large digital basket. But what can you do with these funds in a permissionless context, where anyone can add liquidity to it? Let's explore how DeFi leveraged the idea of liquidity pools.

What is a liquidity pool?

A liquidity pool is a collection of funds locked into a smart contract. Liquidity pools are used to facilitate decentralized trading and lending, as well as many other functions that we will explain later.

Liquidity pools are the backbone of many decentralized exchanges, such as Uniswap. Users called liquidity providers add an equal value of two tokens in a pool to create a market. In exchange for the funds provided, they receive the trading fees of the transactions carried out in the pool, in proportion to their share of the total liquidity.
Since anyone can become a liquidity provider, AMMs have made market making more accessible.

One of the first protocols to use liquidity pools was Bancor, but the concept gained more attention with the release of Uniswap. Other popular exchanges that use Ethereum liquidity pools are SushiSwap, Curve, and Balancer. The liquidity pools on these platforms contain ERC-20 tokens. Similar equivalents on Binance Smart Chain include PancakeSwap,

BakerySwap, and BurgerSwap, whose pools contain BEP-20 tokens.

Liquidity pool vs. order book

To understand what sets liquidity pools apart, let's take a look at the fundamental component of trading: the order book. Simply put, the order book is a collection of the orders currently open for a given market.

The system that matches orders to each other is called the matching engine. Together with the matching engine, the order book is the foundation of any centralized exchange. This model is great for facilitating efficient trading and has enabled the creation of complex financial markets.

Trading in DeFi, on the other hand, involves executing on-chain trades, without a centralized party holding the funds. This presents a problem when it comes to order books. Each interaction with the order book requires gas fees, making it much more expensive to trade.

In addition to this, it also makes the work of market makers extremely expensive. Most importantly, most blockchains don't have the throughput capabilities needed to handle billions of dollars in exchanges every day.

This means that, on a blockchain like Ethereum, an on-chain exchange with the order book model is practically impossible. You can use side chains or layer-two solutions. However, the network in its current form cannot handle this throughput.

Before continuing, it should be noted that there are DEXs that work without problems with on-chain order books. Binance DEX is built on Binance Chain, and is designed specifically for fast and cheap trading. Another example is Project Serum, developed on the Solana blockchain.

However, since most of the assets in the crypto sector are located on Ethereum, it is not possible to trade them on other networks, unless you use some type of cross-chain bridge.

How do liquidity pools work?

Automated Market Makers are a significant innovation that makes on-chain trading possible without the need for an order book. Since no direct counterparty is needed to execute trades, traders can open and close positions on token pairs that would likely be highly illiquid on order book exchanges.

You can think of an order book exchange as a peer-to-peer system, where buyers and sellers are connected by the order book. For example, trading on Binance DEX is peer-to-peer as the operations take place directly between users' wallets.
Trading through an AMM is different. You can think of AMM trading as peer-to-contract.

As we have mentioned, a liquidity pool is a set of funds deposited into a smart contract by liquidity providers. When you trade on an AMM, you don't have a counterparty in the traditional sense of the term. Instead, you run it against the liquidity contained in the pool. In order for the buyer to buy, there must not be a seller at that particular time, as long as there is sufficient liquidity in the pool.

When you buy the new fashion token on Uniswap, there is no seller on the other side in the traditional sense. In reality, your business is managed by an algorithm that determines what happens in the pool. Furthermore, prices are also defined by this algorithm based on the operations carried out in the pool.

Obviously, liquidity has to come from somewhere, and anyone can become a liquidity provider. Therefore, this group could be seen in some sense as your counterpart. However, it differs from the order book model in that you are interacting with the smart contract that manages the pool.

The use of liquidity pools

So far, we have mainly talked about AMM, being the most popular application for liquidity pools. However, as we have already mentioned, cash aggregation is a profoundly simple concept, so it can be used in a lot of different ways.

One of these is yield farming or liquidity mining. Liquidity pools are the foundation of automated yield farming platforms such as yearn, where users add funds to pools which are then used to generate returns.
Distributing new tokens in the hands of the right people is a very difficult problem for crypto projects. Liquidity mining has been one of the most successful approaches. In practice, tokens are algorithmically distributed to users who deposit their tokens in a liquidity pool. After that, the newly issued tokens are distributed in proportion to each user's share in the pool.

Remember, these can also be tokens from other liquidity pools called token pools. For example, if you provide liquidity to Uniswap or lend funds on Compound, you will receive tokens representing your share of the pool. You may have the opportunity to deposit these tokens into another pool and make a profit. These chains can get quite complicated as protocols integrate token pools from other projects into their products.

We can also point to governance as a use case. In some projects, the threshold of token votes needed to submit a formal governance proposal is very high. If the funds are pooled, the participants can support a common cause they feel is important to the protocol.

Another emerging segment in DeFi is smart contract risk insurance. Many implementations of these services use liquidity pools.

Another, even more advanced, use of liquidity pools is tranching. It is a concept borrowed from traditional finance. It involves splitting financial products based on their risks and returns. Basically, these products allow LPs to select customized risk-return profiles.
The issuance of synthetic assets on the blockchain is also based on liquidity pools. Add collateral to a cash pool, link it to a trusted oracle, and you have a synthetic token anchored to any asset. In reality, it is a more complicated procedure, but the basic concept is simple.

The risks of liquidity pools

If you provide liquidity to an AMM, you need to pay attention to a concept called impermanent loss. In short, it is a dollar loss compared to the simple holding strategy when you provide liquidity to an AMM.
If you are providing liquidity to an AMM, you are likely exposed to impermanent loss. Sometimes it can be minimal, in other cases it can be huge.

Another danger to keep in mind are the risks of smart contracts. When you deposit funds into a cash pool, they are in the pool. Therefore, even if technically there are no intermediaries in possession of your funds, the smart contract itself can be considered a custodian. In the event of a bug or flash loan exploit, you could lose your funds forever.
Also, beware of projects whose developers have the ability to change the rules of the pool. Sometimes, developers may have an admin key or other type of privileged access in the smart contract code. This can allow them to potentially do something harmful, like take control of the funds in the pool.

Liquidity pools are one of the core technologies behind DeFi's current technology. They enable decentralization of trading, lending, generating returns and more. These smart contracts enable nearly every component of DeFi, and in all likelihood they will continue to do so for the foreseeable future.

Liquidity pools can be quite complicated and we do not recommend them to beginners.

Chapter 4

Flash Loans

In previous chapters we have often mentioned flash loans, but we have never really explained what they are. In the next few pages we are going to do just that.

However, before we can talk about cryptocurrency flash loans we need to address how standard loans work.

Unsecured loans

An unsecured loan is a loan in which you do not have to provide any collateral. In other words, there isn't an asset that will go to your lender if you don't repay the loan. For example, suppose you really want a $3,000 gold necklace. You don't have the money you need, but you will have it when you get paid next week.

Therefore, you talk to your friend Bob and you explain to him how much you care about this necklace. Bob agrees to lend you the money. Provided, of course, that you pay it back as soon as you receive your salary.

Bob is a close friend of yours, so he didn't ask for a commission when he loaned you the $3,000. Not everyone will be so nice. Bob trusts you and is convinced that you will pay him back. Another person may not know you, so they don't know if you could run away with their money.

Typically, unsecured loans from institutions require some type of credit check. They will analyze your track record to assess your ability to repay the debt. If they see that you have taken out several loans and paid them back on time, they may think you are quite reliable and lend you some money.

At that point, the institution transfers the money to you, with constraints. These constraints are interest rates. To get the money now, you have to accept that you will pay back a higher amount later.

You may already know this model if you use a credit card. If you don't pay a card for a certain period, you are charged interest until you repay your entire balance.

Secured loans

Sometimes a good credit score isn't enough. Even if you have repaid all of your loans on time for decades, you will have a hard time getting large-amount loans based solely on your creditworthiness. In these cases, you will need to provide collateral.

If you ask someone for a large loan, granting it is risky. To reduce the risk, the lender will force you to stake something. Your asset will go to the lender if you fail to repay the loan on time. The idea is that the lender can recover some of the value they have lost. Simply put, this is the collateral.

Suppose you want to buy a $50,000 car. Bob trusts you, but he doesn't want to give you money on an unsecured loan. Instead, he asks you to provide collateral. This could be your jewelry collection. Now, if you don't pay back the loan, Bob can take over your collection and sell it to recoup some of the money he lost.

Flash loans

We can include flash loans in the unsecured category simply because you don't provide any collateral. However, you don't have to go through a credit check or other similar procedure either. You just have to ask the lender if you can borrow $50,000 in ETH and you will be good to go.

Where's the catch? A flash loan must be repaid in the same transaction. This feature is not intuitive, but only because we are used to the format of a normal transaction where the funds move from one user to another. Like when you pay for goods or services, or deposit tokens on an exchange.

However, if you know about Ethereum, you will know that the platform is quite flexible. In the case of a flash loan, you can think of your transaction "schedule" as having three parts: get the loan, do something with the loan, repay the loan. And it all happens in a flash.

We can attribute this to the magic of blockchain technology. The transaction is transmitted to the network, temporarily lending you the funds. In the second part of the transaction, you can perform several actions. Do what you want, as long as the funds return in time for the third part. If not, the network rejects the transaction, so the funds go back to the lender. In reality, as far as the blockchain knows, the lender has always had the funds.

This explains why the lender does not ask you for collateral. The contract to repay it is applied by the code.

What's the point of flash loans?

At this point, you are probably wondering why you should use a flash loan. If all of this happens in a single transaction, you can't buy a Lamborghini, right? Well, that's not exactly the goal. Let's focus on the second part of the transaction described above, where you do something with the loan. The idea is to send the funds to a smart contract (or a series of smart contracts), generate a profit and return the initial loan when the transaction is complete. As you can see, the point of flash loans is to make money.

There are a couple of use cases where this might come in handy. Evidently, you can't do off-chain stuff in this time frame, but you can leverage DeFi protocols to make more money using your loan. The most popular applications of flash loans are in arbitrage, where you take advantage of the price disparities between different trading platforms.

Suppose a token is priced at $10 on DEX A, while on DEX B it costs $10.50. Assuming there are no commissions, buying ten tokens on DEX A and reselling them on DEX B would yield a profit of $5. This type of business won't allow you to buy a private island any time soon, but you can see how it allows you to make money by moving large volumes. If you buy 10,000 tokens for $100,000 and manage to resell them for $105,000, you will have a profit of $5,000.

If you get a flash loan, you can take advantage of arbitrage opportunities like this on decentralized exchanges. Here's an example of what the process might look like:

- Get a $ 10,000 loan
- Use the loan to buy tokens on DEX A
- Resell tokens on DEX B
- Repay the loan and any interest
- Enjoy your earnings

The beauty is that all of this happens in one transaction! However, realistically speaking, transaction fees, coupled with stiff competition, interest rates and slippage, make the margins for arbitrage very slim. You should find a way around the price differences to make the process profitable. When you compete against thousands of other users trying to do the same thing, you won't have much luck.

Flash loan attack

Cryptocurrencies and DeFi are a highly experimental sector. When so much money is at stake, it is only a matter of time before vulnerabilities are discovered. On Ethereum, we saw a striking example of this with

The DAO hack in 2017. Since then, several protocols have suffered 51% attacks for financial gains.

In 2020, two high-profile flash loan attacks saw criminals steal nearly $1,000,000 in value at the time. Both attacks followed a similar pattern. Let's take a look at how they happened.

The first flash loan attack

In the first case, the borrower obtained an Ether flash loan on dYdX, a dApp dedicated to loans. The borrower split this loan and sent it to two other lending platforms: Compound and Fulcrum.

On Fulcrum, the borrower used a portion of the loan to short ETH against wrapped Bitcoin (WBTC). Therefore, Fulcrum had to buy WBTC. This information was passed on to another DeFi protocol, Kyber, which filled the order on Uniswap, a popular Ethereum-based DEX. However, due to Uniswap's low liquidity, the price of WBTC increased significantly, so Fulcrum overpaid for the WBTCs it bought.

At the same time, the borrower secured a WBTC loan on Compound using the remainder of the dYdX loan.

When the price went up, the borrower moved the WBTCs on loan to Uniswap and made a modest profit. Finally, they repaid the loan on dYdX and pocketed the remaining ETH.

It sounds like a lot of work, and it might even be too hard to follow. The point is, the borrower used five different DeFi protocols to manipulate the markets. Incredibly, this all happened within the time frame that the original flash loan was confirmed.

The problem lies in the bZx protocol used by Fulcrum. By manipulating the market, the borrower managed to trick it into believing that WBTC was worth much more than it actually was. A pretty clever idea if you ask us.

The second flash loan attack

That was not a good week for bZx. A few days later, the protocol was hit by another attack. The borrower obtained a flash loan and converted part of it into a stablecoin called sUSD.

However, despite their name smart contracts are not very smart. They don't know how much stablecoins should cost. So when the manager placed a huge order to buy sUSD using the borrowed ETH, the price doubled on Kyber.

bZx believed that sUSD was worth $2 instead of $1. Afterward, the borrower took out a much larger loan of ETH than would normally have been possible on bZx, as their $1 coin had the purchasing power of $2. Finally, the manager repaid the initial flash loan and pocketed the rest.

Are flash loans risky?

Right or wrong, this particular attack model is impressive, because it demonstrates how far the bad guys can go. It is easy to look back at the methods used and say that bZx should have used a different price oracle to obtain data. The reality is that this type of theft is incredibly cheap: it doesn't require a particular investment on the part of the attacker. There was no financial deterrent that could stop them from succeeding.

Traditionally, individuals or groups who want to manipulate the market need huge amounts of cryptocurrency. With flash loans, on the other hand, anyone can become a whale for a few seconds. As we have seen, a few seconds is enough to pocket hundreds of thousands of dollars in Ether.

Looking on the bright side, the rest of the industry will learn from the two attacks. Is it possible that someone else will be able to carry out such an attack now that everyone knows about them? Maybe. Oracles have a number of weaknesses, as seen in the second attack, and they need considerable work to get rid of those vulnerabilities.

All in all, this does not depend on the flash loans and this form of DeFi lending could have many interesting use cases in the future, especially considering the low risks to creditors and debtors.

We have never taken a flash loan and we do not recommend them to you. Please, do not try to cheat this system, as hackers never end up well.

Chapter 5

Atomic Swap

Atomic swaps consist of a technique that allows a quick exchange between two different cryptocurrencies, operating on distinct blockchain networks. This process is based on smart contracts, and allows users to buy and sell coins directly from their personal crypto wallet. In other words, atomic swaps are peer to peer exchanges across different blockchains.

Despite being an innovative technique, the idea of cross-chain trading has been the subject of discussion for many years. Tier Nolan was probably the first to describe a complete atomic swap protocol in 2013. However, in 2012 Daniel Larimer presented a trustless trading protocol called P2PTradeX which many consider to be the prototype of an atomic swap.

In the following years, several developers began experimenting with atomic swap protocols. The available data suggests that the Bitcoin, Litecoin, Komodo and Decred communities have played an important role in this process.

Apparently, the first peer to peer atomic swaps took place in 2014. But it wasn't until 2017 that the technique became known to the general public. This was mainly due to the successful swaps between LTC / BTC and DCR / LTC.

How do atomic swaps work?

Atomic swap protocols are designed to prevent deception by any participant. To understand how they work, let's assume Alice wants to exchange her Litecoin for Bob's Bitcoin.

First of all, Alice deposits her LTCs at the address of a contract that acts as a safe. Upon creating this safe,

Alice also generates a key to access it. She then shares a cryptographic hash of the key with Bob. Bob can't access the LTCs yet because he only owns the hash of the key and not the key itself.

After that, Bob uses the hash provided by Alice to create another contract address, where he deposits his BTC. To claim the BTC, Alice must use the same key and, in doing so, she reveals it to Bob. This happens thanks to a special function called hashlock. This means that as soon as Alice claims the BTC, Bob is able to claim the LTC and the swap is closed.

The term 'atomic' refers to the fact that these transactions take place either entirely or not at all. If one of the participants gives up or doesn't do what they are supposed to do, the contract is canceled, and the funds are automatically returned to their owners.

Atomic swaps can take place in two different ways: on-chain and off-chain. On-chain atomic swaps take place on the network of one of the coins. In the example we just made, on the Bitcoin or Litecoin blockchain. Off-chain atomic swaps, on the other hand, take place on a secondary level. This type of atomic swap typically relies on two-way payment channels, similar to those used in the Lightning Network.

Technically speaking, most of these trustless trading systems are based on smart contracts that use multi-signature and Hash Timelock Contracts.

Hash Timelock Contracts (HTLC)

In addition to being an important part of Bitcoin's Lightning Network, Hash Timelock Contracts (HTLC) are also a key component that makes atomic swaps possible. As the name suggests, they rely on two central functions. A hashlock and a timelock.

A hashlock is what prevents the spending of funds unless a specific data is revealed. A timelock is a function that ensures that the contract can only be executed within a predefined interval. Consequently, the use of HTLC removes the need for trust as it creates a specific set of rules that prevents partial execution of atomic swaps.

Advantages of atomic swaps

The main advantages of atomic swaps are related to their decentralized nature. By removing the need for a centralized exchange or any other type of broker, cross-chain swaps can be performed by two parties without having to trust each other. They also provide an increased level of security as users don't have to trust their funds to a centralized exchange or third party. Instead, exchanges can take place directly from users' personal wallets.

Furthermore, this form of peer to peer trading has much lower operating costs as trading fees are either very low or absent. Finally, atomic swaps make it possible to execute exchanges very quickly, with higher levels of interoperability. In other words, it is possible to trade altcoins directly without using Bitcoin or Ethereum as an intermediary currency.

Limits

There are some conditions that must be met for the execution of an atomic swap, and could present obstacles to the widespread adoption of the technique.

For example, to perform an atomic swap, the two cryptocurrencies must be based on blockchains that share the same hashing algorithm. In addition to this, they must be compatible with HTLC and other programmable features.

Atomic swaps raise user privacy concerns. This is because on-chain exchanges and transactions can be tracked on a blockchain explorer. This allows the easy linking of addresses. A short-term solution to this problem is the use of privacy-focused cryptocurrencies to reduce exposure. However, many developers are experimenting with the use of digital signatures in atomic swaps as a more reliable solution.

The importance of atomic swaps

Atomic swaps have great potential to improve the cryptocurrency industry and have yet to be tested on a larger scale. Cross-chain trading can solve many of the problems that affect most centralized exchanges. Some of these problems include the following.

- Greater vulnerability. Keeping many valuable assets in one place alone makes them vulnerable to cyberattacks. Therefore, centralized exchanges are prime targets for digital theft.

- Poor management of funds and human error. Centralized exchanges are operated by people. If those in important roles make mistakes or if leaders make poor choices regarding the operation of the exchange, users' funds can be compromised forever.

- Higher operating costs. Centralized exchanges have higher trading and withdrawal fees.

- Inefficiency in terms of volume demand. When market activity becomes too intense, centralized exchanges often fail to handle the increased demand. This causes the system to slow down or disconnect.

- Legislation. In most countries, cryptocurrency legislation is far from ideal. There are still many problems surrounding government approval and management.

Although atomic swaps are still quite new and have limitations, this technology is bringing significant changes in interoperability between blockchains and in the possibilities of cross-chain trading. As such, the technology has great potential to influence the growth of the cryptocurrency industry, opening new avenues for decentralization and peer to peer money transfers. It is very likely that atomic swaps will be used more and more in the future, especially within decentralized exchanges.

Chapter 6

NFTs

The creation of Bitcoin introduced the concept of trustless, digital rarity. Before its launch, the cost of replicating something in the digital world was almost nil. With the advent of blockchain technology, programmable digital rarity has become possible and is now used to map the digital world to the real world.

Non-fungible tokens (NFTs), also often referred to as crypto collectibles, further develop this idea. Unlike cryptocurrencies, where all tokens are created equally, non-fungible tokens are unique and limited in quantity.

NFTs are one of the building blocks of a new blockchain-based digital economy. Several projects are experimenting with NFTs for a variety of use cases, including video games, digital identity, licensing, certificates, and artwork. Additionally, they can also allow for fractional ownership of high-value items.

As NFTs are becoming easier to issue, new types of assets are created every day. This chapter will explain what NFTs are, what they can be used for, and how a game called CryptoKitties congested the Ethereum blockchain in late 2017.

What are NFTs?

A non-fungible token is a type of cryptographic token on a blockchain that represents a single asset. It can be an entirely digital asset or tokenized versions of assets in the real world. Since NFTs are not interchangeable with each other, they could function as a proof of authenticity and ownership in the digital world.

Fungibility means that the individual units of an asset are interchangeable and essentially indistinguishable from each other. For example, fiat currencies are fungible, as each unit is interchangeable with any other equivalent individual unit. A ten dollar bill is interchangeable with any other genuine ten dollar bill. This is imperative for an asset that aims to serve as a medium of exchange.

Fungibility is a desirable property for a currency, as it allows for free trade and, theoretically, there is no way to know the history of each individual unit. However, this is not a useful feature for collectibles.

What if instead we could create digital assets similar to Bitcoin, with the difference of a unique identifier for each unit? This would make each of them different from all other units. This is an NFT.

How NFTs work

There are various frameworks for creating and issuing NFTs. The best known of these is ERC-721, a standard for issuing and trading non-fungible assets on the Ethereum blockchain.

A newer and improved standard is the ERC-1155. It allows a single contract to contain both fungible and non-fungible tokens, opening up a whole new range of possibilities. The standardization of NFT issuance enables a higher degree of interoperability, which ultimately benefits users. Basically it means that unique assets can be transferred between different applications with relative ease.

If you want to keep and contemplate your awesome NFTs, you can do it with Trust Wallet. Just like other blockchain tokens, your NFT exists on one address. It is important to note that NFTs cannot be replicated or transferred without the owner's permission. Not even the issuer of the NFT can do that.

NFTs can be traded in open markets, such as OpenSea. These markets connect buyers with sellers, and the value of each token is unique. Of course, NFTs are subject to price changes in response to market supply and demand.

But how can these things have any value? Just like any other precious object, the value is not inherent in the object itself but is assigned by people who believe it to be precious. In essence, value is a shared belief. It doesn't matter whether it's fiat money, precious metals or a vehicle. All these things have value because people believe they have it. This is how every precious object (including NFTs) acquires value.

The use of NFTs

NFTs can be used by decentralized applications to issue unique digital items and crypto collections. These tokens can be a collectible, an investment product, or something else.

The economics of video games are nothing new. Furthermore, considering that many online games already have their own economy, using blockchain to tokenize gaming assets is a simple step forward. In fact, the use of NFT could potentially solve or mitigate the inflation problem common to many video games.

While virtual worlds are already thriving, another interesting use of NFTs is the tokenization of assets in the real world. These NFTs can represent fractions of physical assets that can be stored and exchanged as tokens on a blockchain. This could introduce new and necessary liquidity into different markets, such as works of art, real estate, and rare collectibles.

Digital Identity is also an industry that can benefit from NFT properties. Storing identification and ownership data on the blockchain would increase privacy and data integrity for many people around the world. At the same time, easy and trustless transfers of these assets could reduce friction in the global economy.

The history of CryptoKitties and Ethereum

One of the first NFT projects that gained significant traction was CryptoKitties, a game developed on Ethereum that allows players to collect, breed and trade virtual cats.

Each CryptoKitty can have a combination of various different properties, such as age, race or color. Therefore, each of them is unique, and they cannot be interchanged with each other. Furthermore, they are indivisible, meaning there is no way to divide a CryptoKitty token into multiple parts.

CryptoKitties gained notoriety after congesting the Ethereum blockchain due to the intense activity that rocked the network. As of April 2021, the all-time high for the number of daily transactions on the Ethereum blockchain is still around the height of the popularity of CryptoKitties. It is clear that the game has caused a great impact on the Ethereum network, but other factors have also contributed to this record, including the popularity of Initial Coin Offerings.

While a controversial topic, CryptoKitties is a fun prime example of a blockchain use case that isn't a coin, but something used for recreational and leisure purposes. Collectively, these virtual cats have moved millions of dollars, and some of the rarest units have sold for hundreds of thousands of dollars.

Famous projects using NFT and crypto collectibles

Many projects already use NFTs as collectibles and trade items. Here is a selection of some of the best known.

Decentraland

Decentraland is a decentralized virtual reality world where players can own and trade pieces of virtual land and other in-game NFT items. Cryptovoxels is a similar game where players can build, develop and trade virtual property.

Gods Unchained

Gods Unchained is a digital trading card game where cards are issued as NFTs on the Ethereum blockchain. Since each digital card is unique, players can own and trade them for the same level of ownership as physical cards.

My Crypto Heroes

My Crypto Heroes is a multiplayer role-playing game in which players can level up historical heroes through missions and battles. Heroes and in-game items are issued as tokens on the Ethereum blockchain.

Binance Collectibles

Binance Collectibles are NFTs issued in partnership between Binance and Enjin for special occasions. If you want to collect them, be sure to follow Binance on Twitter and stay tuned for the next giveaways. If you want to participate in an NFT giveaway, follow these steps:

- Download a wallet that supports Ethereum, such as MetaMask.
- Copy your Ethereum address and provide it according to the giveaway rules. You may have to submit it through a form or leave it in a Twitter comment. Be sure to double-check the rules to find out what to do in order to participate.
- If you have won an NFT and it has been distributed, you will see it in the Collectibles tab of MetaMaks. From here, you can sell it in a P2P marketplace like OpenSea.

Crypto Stamps

Crypto Stamps are issued by the Austrian Postal Service and connect the digital world with the real one. These stamps are used to carry mail like any other stamp, but are also saved as digital images on the Ethereum blockchain, making them a digitally exchangeable collector's item.

Digital collectibles open blockchain technology to entirely new possibilities, outside of conventional financial applications. By representing physical assets in the digital world, NFTs have the potential to become a crucial part of the economy in general.

The use cases are numerous, and it is likely that many developers will introduce new and exciting innovations for this promising technology.

We absolutely love NFTs and we hold some Crypto Punks and Hashmasks.

Chapter 7

Elastic Offer Tokens

ecentralized Finance has seen an explosion of new types of financial products on the blockchain. We have already talked about yield farming, Bitcoin tokenized on Ethereum, Uniswap and flash loans. Another interesting emerging segment of the crypto sector includes tokens with elastic offers, or rebase tokens.

The particular mechanism on which they are based allows a lot of experimentation. Let's see how these tokens work.

What is an Elastic Offer Token?

A token with an elastic offer works by expanding or reducing the supply in circulation based on changes in its price. The increase or decrease occurs through a mechanism called rebase. With rebase, the token supply is algorithmically increased or decreased, based on the current price of each token.

In some ways, elastic bidding tokens can be compared to stablecoins. They try to keep a target price, and these rebase mechanisms facilitate the process. However, the key difference is that rebase tokens do so with a mutable offer.

Wait, aren't there a lot of cryptocurrencies already operating with a changing offering? In a certain way, yes. Currently, 6.25 new BTCs are issued with each block. After the 2024 halving, this sum will be reduced to 3.125 per block. It's a predictable rate, so we can estimate how many BTCs will exist next year or after the next halving.

Elastic bidding tokens work differently. As mentioned, the rebase mechanism adjusts the token's offer periodically. Let's say we have an elastic offering token that aims to hold a value of 1 USD. If the price is above 1 USD, the rebase expands the current offer, reducing the value of each token. Conversely, if the price is below 1 USD, the rebase reduces the offer, increasing the value of the token.

What does this mean from a practical point of view? The amount of tokens in users' wallets changes when a rebase occurs. Suppose you own Rebase USD (rUSD), a hypothetical token that tries to hold a price of 1 USD. We have 100 rUSD safe in our hardware wallet. Let's assume the price falls below USD 1. After running the rebase, we will only have 96 rUSD in our wallet, but at the same time, each coin will be worth more than before the rebase.

The idea is that the proportion of your funds to the total offer has not changed with the rebase. If you had 1% of the offer before the rebase, you should still have 1% after the event, even if the number of coins in your wallet has changed. Essentially, you hold your share of the network regardless of the token price.

It is a pretty fascinating subject, because rebase tokens have a lot of potential. Let's take a look at a couple of examples.

Ampleforth

Ampleforth is one of the first coins created with an elastic offering. Ampleforth proposes itself as an unsecured synthetic commodity, where 1 AMPL has a target price of 1 USD. Rebase events happen every 24 hours.

The project was relatively unknown before the introduction of a liquidity mining campaign called Geyser, which was particularly interesting for its duration. The scheme distributes tokens to participants over a 10-year period. Geyser is a great example of how liquidity incentives can create significant interest in a DeFi project.

While technically a stablecoin, AMPL's price chart shows how volatile bidding tokens can be.

It may make more sense to represent tokens with elastic supply in terms of market capitalization. Since the price of individual units is less important, the market cap can be a more accurate parameter of the growth and spread of the network.

Yam Finance

Yam Finance is another elastic offering token that is gaining some popularity. The overall design of the Yam protocol is something of a combination of Ampleforth's elastic offering, Synthetix's staking system, and the fair launch of yearn.finance. YAM is also aiming for a target price of USD 1.

YAM is a community experiment, as all tokens were distributed via liquidity mining. There was no premine, no allocation to founders. In other words, the playing field for acquiring these tokens was the same for everyone through a yield farming program.

As a completely new and unknown project, Yam reached $600 million in locked-in value in its staking pools in less than two days. What may have attracted a lot of liquidity is the fact that YAM's farming was aimed specifically at the most popular DeFi tokens: COMP, LEND, LINK, MKR, SNX, ETH, YFI, and Uniswap's ETH-AMPL LP tokens.

However, due to a bug in the rebase mechanism, a lot more offer than expected has been issued. Afterwards, the project was launched again and migrated to a new smart contract thanks to a joint effort and a community-funded audit. Now the future of Yam is completely in the hands of the owners of YAM.

The risks of Elastic Offer Tokens

Elastic offer tokens are highly risky and very dangerous investments. You should only invest if you fully understand what you are doing. Remember, looking at the price charts won't be very helpful, as the amount of tokens you own will change after rebases.

Sure, this can amplify the gains on the upside, but it can also multiply the losses. If the rebase event happens while the token price is falling, you will not only lose money from the price drop, but you will also own fewer tokens after each rebase!

Being quite difficult to understand, investing in rebase tokens will likely result in a loss for most traders. Invest only in tokens with elastic offers that you understand well. Otherwise, you will not be in control of your investment and will not be able to make informed decisions.

Elastic bidding tokens are one of the must-follow innovations in DeFi. As we have seen, they are coins and tokens that can algorithmically adjust their offer to try to maintain a target price.

Are Elastic Bidding Tokens just an interesting experiment, or will they gain significant popularity? It's hard to say, but there are new DeFi protocol designs under development that seek to further advance this idea.

We have not invested in Elastic Offer Tokens and we do not plan to do it any time soon. The volatility of cryptocurrency is already pretty high, there is no need to add a complicated rebase system to the mix.

Chapter 8

The Coin Burn Process

In previous chapters we have mentioned this process. It is time to dive deeper into what it is and how it influences the economy of cryptocurrencies that do it.

The coin burning process aims to permanently remove coins from the market, reducing the total supply. To explain how this works and why, we will use BNB as an example.

Binance carries out periodic Coin Burn events through the use of a smart contract function known as a burn function. BNB coin burning events are scheduled for each quarter until 100,000,000 BNB tokens are destroyed, which is 50% of the total BNB issued (200,000,000 BNB).

The number of BNB coins to be destroyed is based on the number of operations performed on the exchange over a period of 3 months. Then, at the end of each quarter, Binance destroys BNB based on the overall trading volume.

The burn process

Basically, a token burn event occurs in the following order.

First of all, a holder of the coin invokes the burn function, declaring that they want to 'burn' a certain amount of coins. The token contract verifies that this person actually has the coins in their wallet, as well as checking that they have not declared an invalid number, such as 0 or -5. Only positive numbers are allowed. If the person does not have enough coins, or if the declared number is invalid, the burn will not be performed. If they have enough coins, the coins will be subtracted from the wallet. After that, the total supply of the coin will be updated, and the coins will be eliminated. By performing the burn function, the declared coins are destroyed and become inaccessible.

Some scammy projects, like Safemoon, offer coin burn events to incentivize people to buy their tokens, given the deflationary nature. However, normally scam coins have a gigantic supply in the first place, so coin burns in those cases are just a marketing tactic.

Chapter 9

MetaMask

During the entirety of this book, we have mentioned MetaMask quite a few times. However, if you are just starting out with cryptocurrency, you might find it difficult to set it up for yourself. Therefore, we have decided to dedicate this chapter to a deep explanation of this useful wallet.

Ethereum brought with it the promise of a distributed internet, the long-awaited Web 3.0. An equal playing field characterized by the absence of central points of failure, effective data ownership and decentralized applications.

The infrastructure is gradually taking shape with an industry-wide focus on decentralized finance and interoperability protocols that aim to connect the various blockchains. It is now possible to trade tokens and cryptocurrencies with trustless methods, take out crypto-backed loans, and even use Bitcoin on Ethereum.

For many Ethereum enthusiasts, MetaMask is the go-to wallet. Unlike normal smartphone or desktop software, it comes as a browser extension, which allows users to interact directly with the web pages that support it. In this chapter, we will explain how MetaMask works and walk you through the first steps of using it.

What MetaMask is

MetaMask is an open source Ethereum wallet that supports all kinds of Ethereum-based tokens (such as those using the ERC-20 standard, or non-fungible tokens). Furthermore, you can receive them from others, or buy and trade them with the integrated services of Coinbase and ShapeShift.

What makes MetaMask very interesting is its ability to interface with websites. Using other wallets you should copy and paste payment addresses or scan a QR code on a separate device. With the MetaMask extension, the website simply connects to your wallet, and asks you to accept or decline the transaction.

MetaMask can function like a normal crypto wallet, but its real strength is the smooth interaction with smart contracts and decentralized applications. Let's see how to set it up.

Install MetaMask

The MetaMask wallet can be installed on Google Chrome, Firefox or Brave browsers. It is also available on iOS and Android, but we won't talk about it in detail. In this chapter we will refer to Firefox, but the steps will be more or less identical on each platform chosen.

First of all, you need to visit the official download page on metamask.io. Here you need to select your browser and you will be redirected to the Chrome web store or Firefox add-on site. Click on the button to add the extension to your browser. You may need to grant some permissions before it is up and running. Make

sure you don't have a problem with the level of access
it has on your browser.

Initializing the wallet

You should now see a welcome message, just click on
"Get Started". You will be asked to import a seed
phrase or create a new one. Click on Create a Wallet.
The next page asks if you want to send anonymized
data to help developers improve the app. Select the
option you prefer.

Now you need to create a password. If you are one of
those legendary creatures who really read the terms of
use of the software they use, you can find them by
clicking on Terms of Use. Otherwise, think of a strong
password, tick the box and click Create.

The seedphrase backup

This step is so important that it deserves a chapter of
its own. MetaMask is a non-custodial service, so no
one else can access your funds, not even the MetaMask
developers. Your tokens exist in a sort of encrypted

vault inside your browser, protected by your password. This means that if your computer is lost, stolen or destroyed, no one can help you recover the wallet. Your private keys will be lost forever in cyberspace.

Therefore, it is vital to write down the backup phrase. It is the only way to recover your account if something unfortunate happens. We recommend that you write down the words and store them in two or three different locations. You don't have to bury them in a fire-resistant vault in the heart of the forest, but it sure doesn't hurt.

Funding the wallet

In this chapter, we will refer to the Ropsten testnet. It is a network that works almost exactly like the real Ethereum network, but its units are worthless. These fake tokens come in handy when you're developing smart contracts and want to make sure they don't have vulnerabilities that allow hackers to steal $50 million worth of crypto with two clicks. Every step we perform on this network will be replicable on the real Ethereum network.

To access the Ropsten testnet, click on Main Ethereum Network in the upper right corner and select Ropsten Test Network.

We will use a faucet to receive fake funds to play with.

You can click on the little fox icon at any time to see a pop-up with your MetaMask account information. Move your mouse to Account 1 and click to copy your Ethereum address. Paste it into the form and click on Send me test Ether.
Ethereum transactions are generally confirmed rather quickly, but it may take some time for 1 ETH to arrive in your wallet. Check if you have received it by clicking on the fox in your toolbar.

Once there, you can start interacting with the dApps.

Unlocking the decentralized web

Since we are on a testnet, we don't have such a large choice of applications to use. For a full list of decentralized applications on the mainnet, check out

State of the DApps or Dappradar. You can play video games, buy unique assets, or bet on prediction markets.

MetaMask and privacy

It is important to be careful what you are authorizing. If a website knows your address, it can see all Ether and Token transactions involving your it. Also, it can link it to your IP address.

Some prefer to separate their addresses to avoid overlaps, while others don't care about these risks. The level of privacy you want to achieve is fundamentally up to you. As a general rule, don't grant access to websites you don't trust.

Exchange Ether for DAI

Time to do our first swap. In this example we will convert to DAI, an ERC-20 token that acts as a stablecoin. Like our Ether testnet, this DAI has no real value. Click on Select a token, add the Uniswap

Default List, and select DAI. Alternatively, you can also choose WETH (wrapped ether).

It remains only to enter the amount of ETH we want to exchange. By doing this, we will see an estimate of how many DAI we are about to receive.

MetaMask will ask for your intervention again. In this case, you will need to confirm the transaction before it is created. Make sure the fees are okay when doing this on the mainnet, they can be substantial.

After that, we just have to wait for the transaction to be confirmed.

Where are your tokens?

Your Ether has disappeared, but your account is not showing the tokens. Don't worry, you just have to add them manually.

For the most popular tokens, you can select Add Token in your wallet and search for the name or ticker. For those less known (or those on the testnet), you need to add the contract address. This is an identifier that tells MetaMask where to look for our balance.

MetaMask offers other useful features that we haven't mentioned yet. You can also connect a hardware wallet, create a contact list and, of course, receive and send funds as you would with a normal wallet. Take a look at the settings to customize the extension according to your needs.

Aside from that, the usual security principles apply: MetaMask is a hot wallet, so it runs on an internet-connected device. This exposes you to greater risk than a cold wallet, which is kept offline to reduce the risk of potential attacks.

The MetaMask app

The MetaMask app for Android / iPhone offers a viable solution for interacting with Web3 apps on the go. With many of the same features found on the extension, it integrates a dApp browser to access various decentralized applications at the touch of a button.

The application procedures are very similar to those of the browser extension. You can make direct transfers of Ether or tokens from your wallet, or even interact with Uniswap as we have seen above. MetaMask is a powerful tool for navigating the decentralized web. Currently, there are more than one milion people using MetaMask every single day.

As the Ethereum network develops, applications like MetaMask will undoubtedly become integral components in the bridge between existing technologies and the new cryptocurrency infrastructure.

Chapter 10

Other Wallets

In the previous chapter we have talked about MetaMask. However, there are different types of wallet you can use to store your crypto. Let's take a look at the different solutions you have.

How cryptocurrency wallets work

Contrary to popular belief, crypto wallets do not actually contain cryptocurrencies. Instead, they provide the tools needed to interact with a blockchain. In other words, these wallets can generate the information needed to send and receive cryptocurrencies via blockchain transactions. Among other things, this information contains one or more public and private key pairs.

The wallet also contains a public address, i.e. an alphanumeric identifier generated based on public and private keys. An address of this type is a specific "location" on the blockchain to which coins can be sent. This means that you can share your public address with other people to receive funds, but you don't have to disclose your private key to anyone.

The private key allows you to access your cryptocurrencies, regardless of which wallet you use. So even if your computer or smartphone is compromised, you can still access your funds from another device, as long as you have the corresponding private key. Remember that coins never really leave the blockchain, they are only transferred from one address to another.

Hot wallet vs. cold wallet

As already mentioned, cryptocurrency wallets can be "hot" or "cold," depending on how they operate.

A hot wallet is any wallet connected in some way to the Internet. For example, when you create an account on MetaMask and send funds to your wallet, you are depositing into a hot wallet. These wallets are quite simple to create, and the funds are quickly accessible, making them practical for traders and for those who use crypto frequently.

Cold wallets, on the other hand, are not connected to the Internet. Instead, they use a physical means to store keys offline, which makes them resistant to online cyber attack attempts. As a result, cold wallets tend to be a much safer alternative to storing your coins. This method is also known as cold storage and is particularly suitable for long-term investors.

Software wallet

Software wallets come in different varieties, each with unique characteristics. Most are connected to the Internet in some way. Below you will find brief descriptions of some of the most common and important types of software wallets.

Web Wallet

You can use a web wallet to access the blockchain via a browser interface without having to download or install anything. This includes both exchange wallets and other browser-based wallet providers.

In most cases, you can create a new wallet and set a personal password to access it. However, some providers keep and manage private keys on your behalf. While this may be more convenient for inexperienced users, it is a dangerous practice. If you don't have your own private keys, you are entrusting your money to someone else. To address this problem, many web wallets allow you to manage your keys. Therefore, it is important to check the technical approach of each wallet before choosing the most suitable one for you.

When using cryptocurrency exchanges, you should consider using the available protection tools.

Desktop Wallet

As the name suggests, a desktop wallet is software that you download and run locally on your computer. Unlike some web-based versions, desktop wallets offer full control over your keys and funds. When you generate a new desktop wallet, a file called "wallet.dat" is stored on your computer. This file contains the private key information used to access your addresses, so you should encrypt it with a personal password.

If you encrypt your desktop wallet, you will be prompted to provide the password each time you run the program to authorize the wallet.dat file. If you lose this file or forget your password, you will most likely have lost access to your funds.

Consequently, it is vital that you backup your wallet.dat file and keep it in a safe place. Alternatively, you can export the corresponding private key or seed phrase. By doing this, you will be able to access your funds from other devices, in case your computer stops working or becomes inaccessible in some way.

In general, desktop wallets can be considered more secure than most web versions, but it is important to check that your computer is free from viruses and malware before creating and using a cryptocurrency wallet.

Mobile Wallet

Mobile wallets work similarly to their desktop counterparts but are specifically designed as smartphone applications. This type of wallet is quite practical as it allows you to send and receive cryptocurrencies through the use of QR codes.

As a result, mobile wallets are particularly suitable for daily transactions and payments, making them a viable option for spending Bitcoin, BNB and other cryptocurrencies in the real world. MetaMask is a great example of a cryptocurrency mobile wallet.

However, like computers, mobile devices are vulnerable to malicious apps and malware attacks. Therefore, it is recommended to encrypt your mobile wallet with a password, as well as back up your private keys to protect your funds in case of loss or breakage of your smartphone.

Hardware Wallet

Hardware wallets are electronic devices that use Random Number Generation to create public and private keys. The keys are then stored on the device itself, which is not connected to the Internet. Therefore, hardware-type wallets are cold wallets and are considered one of the safest options.

Although these wallets offer much higher levels of security against online attacks, they could present risks if the firmware implementation is not performed correctly. Additionally, hardware wallets tend to be less user-friendly, and it is more difficult to access funds than it can be with a hot wallet.

You should consider using a hardware wallet if you intend to hold your crypto for a long time or if you have large amounts of cryptocurrencies. Currently, most hardware wallets allow you to set a PIN code to protect the device, as well as a recovery phrase.

Paper Wallet

A paper wallet is a piece of paper on which a public address and its private key are physically printed in the form of QR codes. Scanning these codes allows you to perform cryptocurrency transactions.

Some paper wallet websites offer the ability to download the code to generate new addresses and keys offline. Therefore, these wallets are highly resistant to online cyber attacks and can be considered as an alternative to cold storage.

However, due to the numerous weaknesses the use of paper wallets is currently considered dangerous and not recommended to beginners. If you want to use a paper wallet, it is essential to understand the risks associated with it. An important weakness of paper wallets is that they do not allow you to send partial funds, but only the entire balance sheet in one go.

For example, imagine you generate a paper wallet to which you have sent several transactions, for a total of 10 BTC. If you decide to spend 2 BTC, you should first send all 10 coins to another type of wallet (e.g., a desktop wallet), and spend 2 BTC from there. You can then send the 8 BTC back to a new paper wallet, although a hardware or software wallet would be a better choice.

Technically speaking, by importing the private key of your paper wallet into a desktop wallet and spending only part of the funds, the remaining coins would be sent to a "different address" which is automatically generated by the Bitcoin protocol. If you do not manually set the new address as the address you control, it is likely that you will lose your funds.

Most of today's software wallets handle this on your behalf, sending the remaining coins to an address that is part of your wallet. However, it is important to remember that your paper wallet will be empty after its first outgoing transaction.

The importance of backups

Losing access to your cryptocurrency wallets can be very costly. Therefore, it is important to make backups regularly. In many cases, backing up wallet-dat files or seed phrases is sufficient. Essentially, seed phrases play a very similar role to private keys but are generally easier to manage. If you have decided to add a password, remember to include it in the backup as well.

Chapter 11

Multisig Wallets

There is a special type of wallet that is used by advanced cryptocurrency enthusiasts, because it offers major improvement regarding security. We are talking about multisig wallets and this chapter is going to dive deeper into this topic.

Multisig means multi-signature, a term that describes a specific type of digital signature that allows two or more users to sign documents as a group. As a result, a multi-signature is produced through the combination of several unique signatures. Multisig technology is widespread in the world of cryptocurrencies, but the principle has existed long before the creation of Bitcoin.

In the context of cryptocurrencies, the technology was first applied to cryptocurrency addresses in 2012, eventually leading to the creation of multisig wallets a year later. Multisig addresses can be used in a variety of contexts, but most cases have to do with security issues.

The way they work

To use a simple analogy, we can imagine a safe with two locks and two keys. Alice owns the first key and Bob owns the second key. The only way to open the box is to provide both keys at the same time, so one of the owners cannot open the box without the other's consent.

In practice, it is possible to access funds within a multi-signature address only by using 2 or more signatures. Consequently, the use of a multisig wallet allows users to create an additional level of security for their money. Before continuing, it is important to understand the basics of a standard Bitcoin address, which is based on a single key.

Single-key vs Multisig

Generally speaking, bitcoins are stored in a standard single-key address, so anyone with the corresponding private key is able to access the funds. This means that you only need a key to sign the transactions and that those who have the private key can transfer the coins whenever they want, without the need for authorization from others.

Even though managing a single-key address is faster and easier than a multisig one, it presents a number of problems, especially when it comes to security. By having only one key, the funds are protected by a single point of vulnerability. For this reason, hackers continue to develop new phishing techniques to try to steal the funds of cryptocurrency users.

Furthermore, single-key addresses are not the most suitable option for companies dealing with cryptocurrencies. Suppose that the funds of a large company are stored within a standard address, with a single corresponding private key. This would imply that the private key would be given to a single person or several people at the same time. This is a method which is clearly not very secure.

Multisig wallets offer a potential solution to both problems. Unlike single-keys, funds stored in a multisig address can only be moved when multiple signatures are provided.

Depending on how the multisig address is configured, it may require a different combination of keys. The most common is 2-of-3, where 2 are sufficient to access the funds of a 3-signature address. However, many other variations exist, such as 2-of-2, 3-of-3, and 3-of-4.

There are several possible applications for this technology. Here are some of the most common use cases of multi-signature wallets for cryptocurrencies.

Increase security

By using a multisig wallet, users are able to prevent problems caused by the loss or theft of a private key.

Therefore, even if one of the keys is compromised, the funds remain safe.

Suppose Alice creates a 2-of-3 multisig address and she keeps each private key in a different place or device (e.g., cell phone, laptop, and tablet). Even if her cell phone was stolen, the thief would not be able to access her funds using only 1 of the 3 keys. The same is true for phishing attacks and malware, which are less likely to succeed as hackers would be able to access a single device and a single key.

In addition to cyber attacks, if Alice loses one of her private keys, she can still access her funds using the other 2 keys.

Two-factor authentication

By creating a multisig wallet that requires two keys, Alice is able to establish a two-factor authentication mechanism to access her funds. For example, she might keep a private key on her laptop, and one on her cell phone. By doing so, she would have the guarantee that only someone with access to both keys can carry out a transaction.

However, keep in mind that using multisig technology for two-factor authentication can be dangerous. This is true in the case of a 2-of-2 multisig address. If one of the keys is lost, it will not be possible to access the funds. Therefore, using a 2-of-3 setup or a third-party 2FA service that offers backup codes would be safer. In the case of accounts on exchange platforms, the use of Google Authenticator is strongly recommended.

Escrow transactions

Creating a 2-of-3 multisig wallet allows for an escrow transaction between two parties, Alice and Bob, that includes a third party, Charlie, as a trusted judge in case something goes wrong.

In such a scenario, Alice would deposit the funds, which would be blocked. Thereafter, if Bob provides the goods or services as agreed, the two parties can use their own keys to sign and complete the transaction.

Charlie, the judge, should only intervene in the event of a dispute. At this point Charlie could use a key to create a signature to give the funds to Alice or Bob, based on her decision.

Decision process

A board of directors could use a multisig wallet to control access to company funds. For example, by setting up a 4-of-6 wallet and giving each one a key, no board member would be able to misuse the funds. Consequently, only decisions that have been agreed by the majority could be enforced.

Disadvantages

While multisig wallets are a viable solution to a number of problems, it is important to remember the associated risks and limitations. Setting up a multisig address requires some technical knowledge, especially if you don't want to rely on third party vendors.

Furthermore, given that blockchain and multisig addresses are both relatively new, it may be difficult to seek legal help if something goes wrong. There is no legal custodian of funds deposited in a wallet shared with several people in possession of a key.

Despite some disadvantages, multisig wallets have numerous interesting applications, making Bitcoin and other cryptocurrencies even more useful and attractive. This is especially true for businesses. By requiring more than one signature to transfer funds, multisig wallets provide greater security and allow for trustless escrow transactions. Therefore, it is very likely that this technology will be used more and more in the future.

We have used multisig wallets in the past, when we needed to put an escrow in place. They have worked well for us and we recommend them for those special occasions.

Chapter 12

Initial Coin Offering (ICO)

We have mentioned the term ICO a few times during the course of this book. In this chapter we are going to dive deeper into this topic. Let's get right into it.

An Initial Coin Offering is a fundraising method through the use of cryptocurrencies. It is mainly used for projects that have not yet fully developed their blockchain platform, product or service. Payment is typically made with Bitcoin or Ethereum, but fiat currencies are also accepted in some cases.

Investors participate in the Initial Coin Offerings with the hope that the company will succeed. In fact, this would result in increasing demand and cause an increase in value in the underlying token. In other words, they hope to get a good return on investment as early supporters of this particular project.

How ICOs work

ICOs are often compared to IPOs (Initial Public Offering). However, this comparison is rather misleading. Typically, IPOs are used by established businesses that sell partial ownership shares to raise funds. Instead, ICOs are mainly used as a fundraising mechanism that allows businesses to raise capital for their project in its early stages. Furthermore, investors who buy tokens are not acquiring any ownership in the company.

Typically, tokens distributed in ICOs are created on the Ethereum blockchain, according to the ERC-20 token standard. This means they are ERC-20 tokens. In addition to Ethereum, there are other platforms that support the creation and issuance of digital tokens (e.g. Stellar, NEM, NEO and Waves). Conversely, companies that already have a functioning blockchain often choose to issue digital assets on their platform.

Taking ERC-20 tokens as an example, a company could use Ethereum smart contracts to create and issue their own digital token. The ERC-20 protocol defines a set of rules that the company must follow in order to issue a token on the Ethereum blockchain, and the smart contract ensures that these rules are followed in a trustless way.

Once the founders of the start-up have created their token, they have to convince investors to participate in the ICO. In order to do this, a whitepaper is created that describes the company's goals and how the new ecosystem should operate. The founders could pair this document with a website that offers more information about the people involved in the ICO and why they believe in the success of the project.

The purpose of ICOs

An ICO can be a very effective method of raising venture capital and financing. For start-ups, it allows you to receive funds based on an idea, which may or may not have been tested on the market. Many of these small, unconsolidated businesses would likely fail to raise funds any other way. Traditional financial institutions would not lend capital on the basis of a whitepaper alone. This is especially in the crypto sector, where the lack of regulation has caused reluctance on the part of these institutions.

While new businesses and start-ups make up the majority of ICOs, things are changing. Some established companies are starting to recognize the value of ICOs and the decentralization potential offered by cryptocurrencies. Some of these have organized ICOs to launch new projects on a blockchain-based system in order to raise capital or decentralize their business. This practice is called "reverse ICO."

Can Anyone Do an ICO?

The short answer is yes. With the right guidance, almost anyone could develop a token and write a whitepaper describing its eventual application. However, the company or individuals who do this must create a viable blockchain project. This requires knowledge, skills and experience that not everyone has. It is also necessary to adhere to the complex network of laws and regulations that vary from one jurisdiction to another and which may soon be modified in response to the growing popularity of ICOs.

To organize a successful ICO, the company should be solid and supported by concrete evidence of how the project or idea will work, why it is valid, what it consists of, who needs it and how it can be developed. Selling the idea and convincing investors to buy is a critical phase towards positive results.

The regulation of ICOs

The growing number of ICOs has attracted the attention of regulatory authorities around the world. Nowadays, crypto regulation is a hot topic in the community. Within the US, the SEC and the CFTC are two regulatory institutions that are discussing the regulatory framework for ICOs and cryptocurrencies.

The regulation of the ICO sector is still in its early stages, and there is no uniformity between different countries. On the one hand, too much regulation risks hindering the growth and development of this emerging sector. On the other hand, there are those who argue that regulation would bring greater legitimacy to the space, alleviating the fears of traditional financial institutions that have so far been reluctant towards it. A balanced approach is preferred by those who believe that the crypto ecosystem should not be a financial "wild west", but at the same time it should have enough freedom to operate outside the limits of the traditional financial system.

While some countries, such as China and South Korea, have outlawed all ICOs, the U.S. SEC has issued a detailed statement on the subject, recommending potential investors to apply due diligence before committing to new investments. The SEC also disclosed that some ICOs may qualify as securities, and as such are subject to relevant federal regulations.

The importance of ICOs

ICOs use cryptocurrencies as their primary funding tool and, as such, offer a new avenue for individuals and innovative businesses who want to act differently. The crypto ecosystem is attracting more and more attention thanks to the large capital raised by blockchain start-ups. Despite this, the ICO method could lead to both favorable and unfavorable results. While scams and large public failures negatively impact cryptocurrency reputation, successful activities bring the industry greater authenticity in the public eye.

ICO tokens that see reliability and widespread adoption could eliminate some of the uncertainties that alienate institutions and consumers from the cryptocurrency industry. Although this new investment method has problems to solve, it is considered by many to be a valid alternative to traditional fundraising practices and could become a compelling approach for several companies in the future.

We have invested in some ICOs and they have always been a wild ride. We do not recommend them to beginners or those that have small capitals. Do not play the "angel investor" game in the world of cryptocurrency, it never ends well.

Chapter 13

Initial Exchange Offering (IEO)

In the previous chapter we have discussed the complicated world of ICOs. However, ICOs are not the only way crypto companies have to raise funds. Another popular practice is IEOs and in this chapter we are going to tell you more about them.

Often an IEO is made when a new crypto project wants to launch its cryptocurrency or blockchain product but requires significant capital to do so.

The IEO model differs from the Initial Coin Offering in that it is made possible with the help of a cryptocurrency exchange, such as Binance or Coinbase. Projects can raise funds by engaging the exchange's customer base and launch trading for their token a little later.

There are several thousand cryptocurrencies and blockchain projects in existence or under development. Most projects require some kind of financial incentive to keep developers and contributors involved. Not all projects can count on donations or contributions from generous investors. More often than not, funding is needed during the development phase.
There are many different ways for developers to raise capital. Trying to obtain finance from venture capital investors can be time-consuming. Issuing a project's coins before its launch and keeping them in a treasury is another option, but it often receives criticism from the community.

Choosing to organize an IEO can be an interesting possibility, assuming the developer has an action plan and is willing to develop the vision of the project.

What an IEO is

As the name suggests, an Initial Exchange Offering (IEO) involves using a cryptocurrency exchange to raise funds for a new project. Asset trading is common on these platforms, but it generally only happens after developers have raised funds to start their own projects.

With an IEO, potential investors can buy these assets before they are available on the market. With the help of the exchange that facilitates the sale of tokens, registered users who have provided KYC information will be able to buy tokens before trading on the free market begins.

Since the IEO is facilitated by an exchange, startups that choose this option will need to be serious about their action plan. In most cases, the IEO proposal is subject to strict scrutiny by the exchange involved. In a way, exchanges put their reputation on the line for every IEO they decide to offer.

Organizing an IEO

Even though blockchain technology is relatively new, there are thousands of startups and crypto companies in the industry. Many of these are competing to acquire potential investors via ICO or IEO events.

When the developers of a crypto project decide to organize an IEO, they have to go through a complicated procedure before they can raise the first dollar.

Several requirements must be met for the project team. Having a solid business model, experienced members, a good use case for the technology, and a detailed white paper are absolutely crucial factors. Organizing an IEO is similar to declaring a long-term commitment to the success of the project.

Additionally, they must determine whether the Initial Exchange Offering will have a hard cap or a soft cap. A hard cap guarantees a limit on the amount of money that can be invested. A soft cap sets an initial goal to reach but allows the developers to raise more money later on.

Once these decisions have been made, it is time to choose an exchange platform to carry out the IEO. Binance Launchpad has helped dozens of projects raise the necessary investment capital. Some examples include BitTorrent, Band Protocol , Axie Infinity, Alpha Finance Lab, and WazirX. Other exchanges have launched their own platforms for IEOs, each with their own benefits, requirements and potential drawbacks.

Why blockchain projects choose IEO

Raising funds for a new crypto or blockchain project can be quite difficult. Similar to any other industry, there is a lot of competition to attract investors. Not everyone can successfully attract investment capital with traditional methods.

An IEO can be useful as it targets existing cryptocurrency holders. As the participating exchange helps lend credibility to the fundraising project, there is a certain degree of trust. After all, the exchange is risking its reputation by facilitating the IEO. However, all interested parties should carry out extensive research before making any financial commitment.

For projects looking to raise money with the help of an exchange, an IEO is a reliable option. Most Initial Exchange Offerings reach their funding goal very quickly, depending on the vision and use cases involved. Furthermore, the project token will be listed on the exchange at the end of the sale.

IEO vs. ICO

On paper, the concept of the IEO could be similar to that of the ICO. During the ICO bubble on Ethereum in 2017-2018, ICOs were organized practically every day. Many projects raised millions of dollars, but there were also a lot of deceptive offers, as well as outright scams. With no one openly "examining" ICOs, the concept eventually evolved into the IEO, which many consider more reliable. Many ICOs have broken US security laws, resulting in various lawsuits and refunds to investors.

Participating in an ICO entailed significant risks. Investors had to send Bitcoin or Ether to a smart contract or website and hope to receive their tokens. Anyone with basic smart contract knowledge and web development skills could create a shiny website with a promising roadmap and start raising money. It was far from ideal and carried a huge risk to anyone investing in ICOs.

IEOs largely mitigate these risks. Investors send money through exchange wallets, instead of sending it directly to the project. Dishonest projects or teams with poor business skills will not be able to conduct a successful IEO, due to very stringent requirements.

Furthermore, an IEO has lower risks and more flexibility than ICOs. The listing of the token on the exchange organizing the sale is guaranteed. For investors, this allows them to close the position whenever they want.

The risks and opportunities of an IEO

While each IEO is reviewed by the exchange, no investment is risk-free. It is possible that the fundraising project will not be able to realize its vision. This can affect the price of the token, regardless of its value during the IEO.

That said, IEOs can also present favorable investment opportunities. Having the ability to buy tokens in advance knowing that they will be listed on markets with good liquidity can create good opportunities. However, not all IEO tokens will increase in value once trading begins.

The lower frequency of IEOs has helped eliminate some of the less recommendable projects in the crypto and blockchain industry. Even if no method is foolproof, it appears that IEOs are at least on the right track.

Just because the IEO exists doesn't mean everyone should invest in these offerings. It is always recommended to do your own due diligence, regardless of how companies and projects raise capital. Contributing funds to an IEO offers benefits, but the risks cannot be ignored.

We like to participate in IEOs only when they are held on an exchange we trust. Stay away from shady exchanges that pretend to offer the next 100x coin. The exchange should be impartial and not advertise the IEO too aggressively.

Chapter 14

Decentralized Exchanges (DEXs)

Initial exchange offerings can be done on decentralized exchanges as well. In this chapter we explain what they are and how they work.

Since the early days of Bitcoin, exchanges have played a vital role in matching cryptocurrency buyers and sellers. Without these forums that welcome a global user base, we would end up with much less liquidity and no way to agree on the correct price of assets. Traditionally, centralized operators have dominated this field. However, with the rapid evolution of available technologies, more and more tools for decentralized exchanges continue to emerge.

Definition of decentralized exchanges

In theory, any peer-to-peer exchange could constitute a decentralized exchange. In this chapter we are mainly interested in a platform that emulates the functions of centralized exchanges. The key difference is that its backend exists on a blockchain. Nobody takes custody of your funds, and you don't have to trust the exchange to the same extent as centralized alternatives.

How a centralized exchange works

With the typical centralized exchange, you deposit your funds. When you deposit a cryptocurrency, you give up its control. Not from a usability point of view, as you can still use it for trading or withdraw it, but from a technical point of view: you can't spend it on the blockchain.

You don't have the private keys associated with the funds, so when you withdraw your coins, you need to ask the exchange to sign a transaction on your behalf. When trading, transactions don't take place on-chain. In fact, in this case the exchange only modifies users' balances in its database.

The overall procedure is incredibly optimized because the slowness of the blockchains does not hinder trading, and it all happens within the system of a single entity. It's easier to buy and sell cryptocurrencies, and you have more tools at your disposal.

This is possible by sacrificing independence. In fact, you have to entrust your money to the exchange. As a result, you expose yourself to some counterparty risk. What happens if the team runs away with your hard earned BTC? What if a hacker paralyzes the system and drains the funds?

For many users, this is an acceptable level of risk. They simply rely on reputable exchanges with excellent records and precautions to mitigate data breaches.

How a decentralized exchange works

DEXs are similar to their centralized counterparts in some respects, but noticeably different in others. First of all, there are different types of decentralized exchanges available to users. The common theme between them is that orders are executed on-chain and that users don't sacrifice custody of their funds at any point in the process.

Despite the considerable work done on cross-chain DEXs, the most popular platforms revolve around assets on a single blockchain.

Order book on-chain

In some decentralized exchanges, everything happens on-chain. Each order is recorded on the blockchain. This is probably the most transparent approach, as you don't have to trust a third party to pass orders and there's no way to obfuscate them.

Unfortunately, it is also the least practical. Since you are asking every node in the network to register the order forever, you end up paying a commission. You have to wait for a miner to add your message to the blockchain. Therefore, it could take a while to see your transaction go through.

Some identify front running as a flaw in this model. Front running occurs in markets when an insider is aware of a pending transaction and uses this information to place a trade before the transaction is processed. The front runner takes advantage of information unknown to the public. Generally speaking, this practice is illegal.
Obviously, if everything is published on a global ledger, there are no front running opportunities in the traditional sense. Instead, it is possible to launch a different type of attack, where a miner sees the order before it is confirmed, and has their order added to the blockchain first.

Examples of on-chain order book models include the Stellar and Bitshares DEXs.

Off-chain order book

DEXs with off-chain order books are still decentralized in some respects, but it must be recognized that they have a greater degree of centralization than the previous category. Instead of recording orders on the blockchain, they are stored on another server.

You may find a centralized entity with full control of the order book. If this entity is dishonest, it could deceive the markets to some extent (through front running or order forgery). However, you would still take advantage of the non-custodial solution.

The 0x protocol for ERC-20 tokens and other standards on the Ethereum blockchain is a good example of this type of DEX. Instead of acting as a single DEX, it provides a participant framework known as a relayer to manage off-chain order books. Using 0x smart contracts and other tools, it is possible to tap into a combined liquidity pool and transmit orders between users. The operation is performed on-chain only when the two counterparties are combined.

These approaches are better in terms of usability than on-chain order book structures. They don't face the same speed limits, as they don't use the blockchain to the same extent. However, the trade must be adjusted to it, so the off-chain order book model remains inferior to centralized exchanges in terms of speed.

Off-chain order book implementations include Binance DEX, IDEX, and EtherDelta.

Pros of DEXs

No KYC

Compliance with KYC / AML measures are the norm for many exchanges. For legislative reasons, individuals are often required to present identification and proof of residence.

This process is an accessibility problem for some users. What if you don't have valid documents available? What if the information is disclosed in some way? Since DEXs are permissionless, no one checks your identity. All you need is a cryptocurrency wallet. However, there are certain legal requirements when DEXs are partially managed by a central authority. In some cases, if the order book is centralized, the group managing it must comply with the rules.

No counterparty risk

The main advantage of decentralized cryptocurrency exchanges is the fact that they do not own client funds. Therefore, even catastrophic incidents like the hack against Mt. Gox in 2014 could not endanger funds or reveal sensitive user information.

Unlisted tokens

Tokens not listed on centralized exchanges can still be traded freely on DEXs, as long as there is supply and demand.

Cons of DEX

Usability

Realistically, DEXs are far less user-friendly than traditional exchanges. Centralized platforms offer real-time operations unaffected by the timing of the blockchain. For beginners who are not familiar with non-custodial cryptocurrency wallets, CEXs offer a more forgiving experience. If you forget your password, you can simply reset it. However, if you lose your seed phrase, your funds are lost in cyberspace.

Trading volumes and liquidity

The trading volume on DEX is nothing compared to that on CEXs. Perhaps more importantly, CEXs tend to have higher liquidity as well. Liquidity is a measure of how easily you can buy or sell assets at a reasonable price. In a highly liquid market, bid and ask prices present little difference, indicating great competition between buyers and sellers. In an illiquid market, you will have a harder time finding someone willing to trade the asset for a reasonable price.

DEXs are still relatively new, so they don't always provide supply or demand for the crypto assets you want to trade. You may not be able to find the trading pair you want, and in any case the assets may not be priced appropriately.

Commissions

Commissions aren't always higher on DEXs. However, they can be, particularly when the network is congested or if you're using an on-chain order book.

Over the past few years, many decentralized exchanges have emerged, each developed on the basis of previous attempts to optimize the user experience and build more powerful trading platforms. Ultimately, the idea seems to align perfectly with the etho of self-determination: as with cryptocurrencies, users don't have to rely on a third party.

Conclusion

Congratulations on making it to the end of this book, we hope you found some useful insights to take your cryptocurrency trading skills to the next level. As you should know by now, the world of cryptocurrency is extremely complicated and there is a new "opportunity" every way you look. However, our experience tells us that only by taking things seriously and having a proper plan you can develop your investing skills to the point that you can actually accumulate wealth.

Our final advice is to stay away from the shining objects that the world of cryptocurrencies offers you every day. Simply study the world of cryptocurrencies in depth and when you feel ready try to invest a little bit of money. Analyze your results, improve your money management skills and become the master of your emotions.

As you can see, there are no shortcuts you can take. Easy money does not exist. What exists is the possibility to start from zero and work your way up to become a professional cryptocurrency investor. The journey might be difficult, but it is certainly worth it.